THREE HE

THE WHEELHOUSE

The True Story about a Boy and His Dogs

A Memoir

A NOVEL BY

DREW GLICK

Learn more about Drew, The WheelHouse and the documentary film series (based on the WheelHouse novels), Twice As Strong by visiting:

www.koffeescreations.com

THE WHEELHOUSE

The True Story About a Boy and His Dogs

Copyright 2016, 2017. 2020 by Drew Glick

All rights reserved

In loving memory of:
SASHA GLICK

There is no greater love then the one you gave me.
There is no greater pain then the one I feel without you.

In loving memory of:
GABBIE GLICK

As I stared into the abyss and watched my death you pulled me back and freed my heart from the demons possessing it.

A special thanks to:

Tufts University, The Bidawee Support Group, The Long Island Veterinary Specialists & Lefferts Animal Hospital.

A very special thanks to:

Joel & Carol Glick, Marcie & Mike Littman, Max & Jesse Littman, Steven Glick, Adam Haney, Jackie Watson, Lois Nosowitz, Irving Morrison, Willie Cedeno, Madea D. Berkman, Joyce Sabella, Elizabeth Anilionis, Stephanie LaFarge, Gabrielle Badell.

Upcoming Releases by Drew Glick:

The WheelHouse: Part II: Death of a White Knight

Future Releases by Drew Glick:

The WheelHouse, Pt. 1.5: The Missing Pieces
The WheelHouse: Part III: EndGame: The Final Chapter
Vagabond Knights: Trilogy of Chaos: Complete Edition
Lords of Annwn: Book One: The Four Kingdoms
Vagabond Knights: The Golden Palace
Valkyrie Princess: Mission: M.E.S.S.I.A.H.

I would like to extend a special thank you to my friend, Eric Hunn for the hand drawn cover design he did for this book.

Eric, you never cease to amaze me.

"Once you have had a wonderful dog, a life without one, is a life diminished."

- Dean Koontz

A LETTER FROM HELEN

Dear Drew,

I have finished your book, *The WheelHouse: The True Story About a Boy and His Dogs* and I wanted to send you this letter to let you know how impressed I am with you [and The WheelHouse]. You describe your dogs as your daughters and feel that you were changed by them being in your life. You talk about how you had to stay alive for them even when there was a part of you that wanted to die. Dogs harbor the epitome of love and it is this love that anchored you three together even in the toughest of times; you gained better awareness about who you were, what you need to do in this life, which seems to be sharing the knowledge that love is what is important and that there is a superior being that helps us on our human level achieve that goal. Throughout your book you share your emotional reactions to your experiences with the dogs with an awareness that these emotions were causing you suffering. There was anger that others did not understand when it came to your "daughters", and you judged them based on that difference. I have heard that there is a Native American belief that a disabled person is born into the tribe to determine how others will treat him to identify their character. It seems to be a similar pattern for you to use your dogs as a measuring tool about the character of others. It is not a bad tool to see how people react to a soul - be it human or animal - that is less powerful than others. It goes with the belief "That which you do to the least of my brethren, you do to me..." The book was very interesting and clearly a major part of your daughters' legacy to not just you, but many others. Good luck on your journey and I hope you continue to share your girls' story with others.

- Helen Zimniewicz

BUILDING THE WHEELHOUSE

This book took me nearly two years to complete (and even today is still undergoing numerous edits and alterations). As I started to write this book I did so with no solid foundation; no start, middle or end, and relied simply on the idea that it [this book] would be a "memoir," and not an all-out story which would chronicle each and every day that I spent with my two daughters, Sasha and Gabbie. Though, as you can imagine I soon changed the premise of the book drastically and did the exact opposite of what I just described. In fact, I combined both ideas into a unique and coherent novel. Yet, it [this book] can also be misleading, vague, and, sometimes downright complicated to understand. Simply put: this book will make no sense to you, the reader if you are closed minded, or, even, scared to admit that our world, universe even is a facade; a makeshift prison of sorts which we are all born into but very few of us can ever escape.

Creating a world which is has never been seen and one which is believed by many to be nothing but outrageous claims inspired by moments of desperation in which I, myself underwent a psychotic break of sorts (as many people later called it) was a complicated and time consuming task solely due to the allegations against me that I was losing my mind due to the events herein unfolding as one would fold a napkin on their lap. Therefore, I had to be careful as not to write this book in a fashion which would only later add credence to the claims being used to discredit my work.

However, the world you are now about to enter is open to us all; it is ageless and full of incredible wonder that will surely have your chin hit the floor and your eyes bulging wide from their sockets as you gaze upon your majestic surroundings which will surely fill you with a divine glow. I reveal this truth to you, the reader because right now at this very moment the walls are closing in around you; your prison cell is becoming smaller and smaller with every breath you take. You see, I spent nearly forty years of my life trying desperately to understand why we, the human race exists here on planet Earth in the first place, and why so many other worlds are barren and unlivable? Finally, after all that time I discovered the reasons why and it was shocking!

These discoveries can only be accomplished, however by an individual who is ready and able to accept that what they see, feel and believe is a lie; an elaborate tale which has been told us for only one reason…so that we may chose, if we wish to do so at all uncover our purpose; a purpose which begins and ends with the question of whether or not we are worthy? Yet, the question you should be asking is worthy of what? Could it be true that our ultimate destiny is hidden within the construct of a grand lie that few of us will ever agree exists or, even, unveil for what it truly is - a rite of passage…Oops! It seems that I may have misconstrued this part of the book and turned it into some sort of bible study class. Let me stop right here…besides there will be plenty of time for me to enlighten you about God, the universe, the meaning of life and so on in due time.

I hear you saying, "Drew, just get on with it already!" Okay. Fine. Have it your way. To understand this book in its entirety you must not see it [this book] for what it is – a book, but rather something which goes well beyond the scope of normal, everyday thinking; you must open your mind to a new way of viewing the world in which we live, seeing it as not as you would a globe of merely dirt and dust but a stepping stone to world beyond human imagination; where thought is alive and full of wonderous substance, substance that connects each and every one of us not simply on the physical plain but as well to the spiritual.

This book does above all else reveal how my two daughters Sasha and Gabbie empowered me in ways which may seem at first glance to be impossible. You will certainly say, "Drew, they're only dogs!" and I will reply, "Dog spelled backwards is GOD, is it not?" Then you will chuckle and remark, "Maybe you're just desperate for there to be a connection of some kind?" I will think about your remark then softly reply in a calm tone of voice and answer your question with a question of my own. "Take a look at the world around you and tell me where you don't see God?" I will then pause momentarily before continuing to say, "God…" I will clear my throat and hesitate but only briefly. After a few moments I will continue to speak while all the while staring into your eyes and trying hard to peer into your soul, "…is in the trees. He, God is in the rocks. He lives in all of us, even, dogs." Yet, nothing I say will convince you otherwise. You have already made up your mind, haven't you?

Maybe I am misjudging you? Perhaps you already know where God lives? Maybe you too have seen His presence each time you gaze out into an open field? Or maybe you see Him when you stare at your reflection while hovering over the glassy surface of a puddle of water? Still, who am I to tell you what to believe? With that being said I want to add that it is a sad fact is that we, humanity look up into the clear blue sky with the hopes of finding Him. Yet, the shocking revelation that will inevitably blindside you like a tractor trailer truck which suddenly jackknifed on the highway and sideswiped your brand-new BMW, is that He, God can be found much closer than you know.

Over the course of 2018/19 I made varying changes to this book; omitted some chapters and changed others, added more defining characteristics to help create a grander vision of what was occurring at a specific moment in time where the story shifted from being good too bad to worse. The reasons for these changes were obvious to some but overall, I felt that the book was in some regard or another "rushed" to completion and never truly reviewed for the content which at times could seem irrelevant to the overall story.

Let me reiterate that this story if you will, or tale as I like to call it is not about me even though I use my experiences, my life as a way to set a precedent for others and also to help further express the importance of my dogs, all dogs as a matter of fact and their importance in helping to correct various behaviors by humankind which are neither instinctive or primitive but rather learned due to the nature of the world in which we live. Many would agree that dogs are the epitome of love, loyalty and compassion which are put on earth for the benefit of all creatures whether big or small. For that reason and that reason alone, I wrote this book to the best of my ability no matter how long it took me to do so because only this book can genuinely show you, teach you rather what it means to be human by seeing humanity through the eyes of a dog.

Now that you better understand the alterations which have taken place from one version of this book to another what do you say I take into my Wheelhouse, and reveal to you the unseen world which even now beckons you? So, are you ready to take journey into Hell? Can you handle being trapped in Oblivion with no way to escape? Though, this story is not all bad for as the old saying goes there can be no good without evil. No light without dark. No Heaven without Hell. What if I could show you a glimpse of Heaven? Would you want to peer into the eyes of God himself or would you shy away in fear that you are not worthy?

All these things and more you will surely see or read about throughout this boo that much is certain. If you replied "yes" to any of the above then allow me to thank you but also give you a final warning; a warning that if you take lightly may very well backfire. Fair? Still want to go? Then consider yourself warned as I tell you one last time to not take this journey lightly. By doing so you may discover the true nature of who and what you really are…Don't look so surprised. Not everyone is ready to face their true self; to confront their inner demons but should you be one of the rare few who fear nothing only fear the wrath of the God almighty then brace yourself and hold on tight because it's gonna be a bumpy ride. But, don't worry none of this is real right?

Surely, I must be exaggerating the forthcoming tale and thus there can be no doubt in anyone's mind that I am surely mixing fact with fiction? Am I? Though, what does it matter, I mean it's just a book after all, right? Or is it?

A NOTE FROM THE AUTHOR

Do not mistake this book for a "wannabe" version of, "Marley and Me"; it is nothing of the sort. This book features profanity and imagery that some readers may find offensive, and as much as I hate to admit it this book is not intended for readers under the age of seventeen. Though, that does not mean that it [this book] is not worth reading. It may in fact be more worthwhile then you know. I say this because if you or someone you know was (or is) like I once was - ignorant - then this book may very well save your life.

It is obvious to me as an author that there are only one of two reasons that I can think of why you picked up this book. First, you read the sleeve (or first few pages) and something told you that you would enjoy reading it? Or, second because you're a dog lover? If I had to guess I would determine that you bought this book (or received it from a friend) because you are in fact connected to animals (dogs specifically) just as much as I am? This trait is what I assume separates you from the vast amount of other people who are easily suckered into an "impulse" buy because of an attractive book cover. I'm correct, aren't I? Over the years I have found many reasons to write books, but no reason has been more compelling than that which made me write this one - my dogs. Some people (or readers) may find that reason corny or just plain dumb? The truth is that writing about my dogs helps me to cope with recent events which even at this very moment haunt and confuse me while at the same time fill me with happiness and joy. Sounds like a contradiction, doesn't it?

I began writing when I was in my late twenties; twenty-six years old, I believe? At first, I had no idea why I wrote what I did? All I knew was that something was "calling" to me and in way guiding my words as I put them down on paper. Those people that know me say that each time I sit before my computer to write I "transform." I used to scoff at their remark and refused to believe that I was capable such a feat? Yet, even today I am filled with a strange sensation each time I re-read the manuscripts I have tucked away in a folder on my external hard drive titled: *My Life's Work*. Inside this folder are dozens of literary works (many unfinished) that, at first glance seem to be written by someone other than myself. Often I find myself repeating, "Who wrote this? This is kick ass!" But then a recent memory enters my mind where I recall being awake at four o'clock in the morning while in a lucid state of utopia writing one page after another desperate to complete the next chapter of the book.

Some readers may or may not be able to relate to how it feels to be an author? It is a life that requires an extraordinary amount of sacrifice. When you think about writing a two-hundred-page novel (or even one that's a mere one hundred pages) you must also think about how many words are on each page. Let's assume that this one page you are now reading has ninety-five words. Now, try and determine how many words are in the book (and please ignore the fact that I told you already). Then, if you're excellent in math (which I'm not) calculate the amount of time it would take to write each page. If you successfully concluded how much time an author must invest into one book alone then surely you can imagine that in order to write a book (in under six months) an author must be diligent and write for no less than nine to twelve hours a day.

Most authors are "starving artists" so if they are going to write a complete novel then he or she must learn to balance both their personal and professional life while trying not to become homeless; very few ever can. I make this point to you, the reader to help you understand the dedication and commitment I have to this book (and my other books as well). Yet, this novel means more to me then the majority of my previous ones; published or unpublished. I sit here each day writing while continuing to write and all the while reading what I have written only to have to re-write it again because I am dissatisfied with some of the content.

As redundant as this may sound, I want to remind you that I endure these tasks for only two reasons: Sasha and Gabbie. I do not write this book for me and I certainly do not write this book under the illusion that I am using their story (Sasha and Gabbie) as a means to generate income. If during the time I spend writing this book I end up homeless on the streets of New York, then so be it. My two dogs are my everything. They mean more to me then I mean to me. Their legacy is something that only I can tell you. Therefore, I have spent the last two years tirelessly writing about them; recalling events from the very first day I brought them home, to the struggles we endured together, to the laughs and fun we shared, to the tragic events that I regrettably exposed them to, and, of course, the unconditional love they continued to show me even when I didn't deserve it.

This book is a testament to the human spirit, which was made stronger, even, unbreakable solely because of two amazing creatures who could not speak nor walk upright who committed their very existence to my well-being; two creatures who showed me the path out of Hell and into Heaven. They alone saved me from a fate worse than death. For over a decade they struggled with me, cried with me, slept with me and, cuddled with me even when I was a complete asshole, and undeserving of their love; they are my daughters; my heart and soul, and my purpose for existing on this earth. I love them no less than a member of my family.

For those readers who may be either a dog owner or just a dog lover I want you to know that you are not alone. Until recently I had no idea that there were dozens, if not hundreds of support groups (and numerous organizations such as Paw to Heart) who are out there waiting for your phone call. Most of these men and women are volunteers who in some regard have had similar experiences as the rest of us. It is important that you know about these groups (and organizations) because no matter how strong you think you may be one day you may need them just as much as I have.

I want to say that I am thrilled that you have chosen to read this book. I hope that you will find it to be an inspiring tale about life, love and never-ending happiness? Should you be willing I ask that you pass it along to a friend or family member to help me continue the legacy of my two beloved dogs who have kept me strong. I hope that as you come to the final pages of this book you will see what I have seen in my "pack" in your own? I know that it is not possible for every reader to write a story about their dogs and the experiences they had. Yet, I encourage you to find your own means to immortalize your dogs (or any pet) as you see fit. I ask you to be strong and never allow anyone to mock or ridicule your love for the animals who have given you (or rather us) more than most of the humans in our lives have.

I do want to add that if you don't have a dog, get one! You will be glad you did because even when you feel like you are being held back, pinned down and being driven to your breaking point you will realize as I did that the dog you choose to love will always love you back no matter who you are or where you come from. Finally, I want to say to those people out there who have come to my aid during my time of need (and there are too many of you to list here) that your support and love has enabled me to write this book during a time when I thought I would be unable to. I am eternally grateful for all you have done for me and my two beloved daughters, Sasha and Gabbie.

To all my readers, fans, family and friends alike I wish you all the best of luck, and hope that every endeavor you undertake is a prosperous one? I also want to take a moment to recognize those people who recently came into my life and who read this book and others. Your comments and feedback, support and constructive criticism have helped me to bring to fruition my life's work in ways I never thought possible. I thank you all for your kind words, generosity and love throughout over the years has helped me to remain strong, steadfast and, on numerous occasions stubborn wherein I never faltered in my belief that anything is possible.

May the force be with you,

Drew Glick

Drew Glick

THE RAINBOW BRIDGE

There is a bridge connecting Heaven and Earth.
It is called the Rainbow Bridge because of its many
colors. On the other side of the Rainbow Bridge
there is a land of meadows, hills and valleys
with lush green gardens.

When a beloved pet passes away, he or she travels
to this place. There is always food and warm spring
weather. The old and frail become young again.
They play all day with each other.

There is only one thing missing. They are not with
their special person who loved them on earth. So,
each day they run and play until the day comes when
one suddenly stops playing and looks up! The nose
twitches! The ears are up! Their eyes are staring.
And this one suddenly runs from the group.

You have been seen, and when you and your special
friend meet, you take him or her in your arms and
embrace. Your face is kissed again, and you look
once more into the eyes of your trusting
friend - your dog.

Then you cross over the Rainbow Bridge together,
never again to be separated.

- Author Unknown

WELCOME TO MY WHEELHOUSE: THE WHAT, WHY, HOW AND WHERE

PT. 1:
THE WHAT

The Urban Dictionary defines a Wheelhouse as: *Anything that can be acted on with confident success.* However, that doesn't necessarily answer the question, "What is a WheelHouse?" now does it? If you were to go outside and ask an average person what they thought a Wheelhouse was they would undoubtedly furrow their brow and look at you in confusion. Some people may even reply, "Isn't that the place over there on the corner that changes flat tires in under thirty minutes or your money back?" More often than not you will get uneducated answers, ridicules remarks or even childish responses.

To be blunt a Wheelhouse is nothing less than a state of being, or better yet, a state of awareness. However, it will seem that no matter intelligent your explanation may sound many people will continue to mock the ideology of a WheelHouse, and may even call you "crazy" or "insane" when you begin to describe to them "what" a WheelHouse is and its overall purpose.

I have always tried to decipher the behavior of people; from their small mannerisms to their bulging eyes as I tell them about my WheelHouse. They seem shocked and even appalled that I would fabricate or as some people claim "lie" to them about the only place where I have ever truly felt safe and free of pain and anguish. More often them not I will ask them, "Do you believe in Heaven?" And, as you can surely assume, they then almost immediately respond with, "Yea, why?" I then continue with my barrage of questions, asking, "Have you ever seen Heaven?" I smirk as I listen to them to state the obvious, "No..." I will then interrupt them and jab my index finger in stabbing motion at their chest and say, "Then you are a fool to not believe that a WheelHouse is a real thing."

Following this brief argument, the conversation then becomes heated and it is then that I am confronted by the inevitable. I am unwillingly drawn back into another waste of time which takes the form of a useless debate where my "opponent" insists that Heaven is real but that a WheelHouse is a human fantasy with no real merit of any kind. No matter how long I attempt to hold back my frustration I soon find emotions flaring up and eventually exploding like a grenade. I then attempt to end my conversation with a sarcastic yet wise remark that goes something like this, "You believe in Heaven because scripture tells you that it is a place of wonder; a place where God waits for your arrival; a place where everlasting peace and happiness surround you. But you have never seen it nor spoken with anyone who has and still you believe it is real. Ask yourself why?"

After a few moments of intense silence, I tell them, "You believe in Heaven because you are afraid not to..." Yet, before continuing I stare into the other persons face and look them up and down while watching their body language. I will then continue, "But, what if Heaven was inside you? Inside all of us as a matter of fact?" Then, the other person becomes intrigued and I can tell they are more attentive to my words. "And what if to get to Heaven you had to go to Hell? What if all you experienced was a test of sorts? A test that requires an incredible amount of sacrifice, and, even pain. Would you still want to see Heaven?" Then, they squint their eyes and ready a question, but I refuse to let them speak. "You see," I say. "Heaven is not a place but rather a state of mind." It is then that they realize what I have been telling them all along. Still they don't quite understand. Do you?

PT. 2:
THE WHY

When writing this book, I opened many doors inside my Wheelhouse and brushed away the cobwebs and dust hoping to find memories which I have long forgotten. I forced myself to go back to a time when I first began my search. What was I searching for? Well, the simple answer would be - God. For years I looked up into the clear blue sky and shouted His name. I sobbed in silence hoping that somehow, someway He would intervene and take away my plight and fill my heart with peace. Instead, He chose me to be a protector who's only purpose was to provide safe haven for His two angels that fell to earth.

As I look back on how it all began, I come to see that it wasn't me who was protecting anyone but rather quite the opposite. The revelation which came to me without warning was that no one can conquer life without assistance from others and sometimes these "others" are not human at all. In fact, the word of God states, "When two or three are together I am in the middle." In essence the reasons why a WheelHouse is part of the human psyche is simple - to allow the human mind to understand what lies beyond our feeble way of thinking. You see, The WheelHouse is a gateway of sorts. Actually, now that I think about it The WheelHouse is a divine transit system that allows us to cross over and step into realm that we, the human race has dubbed - Heaven.

I want to continue by saying to those of you who have <u>not yet</u> discovered the secret of the WheeHouse to proceed carefully and to never underestimate such a magical place just because it is imaginary. Or is it? The WheelHouse has great power and it can sometimes be frightening experience for those people who think they can overpower such an ancient place with muscle and grit. The primary dilemma is that people rely on their rage, hate and anger to influence change in their personal lives and the lives of others, and inevitably to change the world. There is a bit of truth to be said about people who use their rage and anger as a weapon. However, there are two kinds of rage and endless forms of anger. Using the right one at the right time and for the right reason can and will change the world. However, explode like a grenade solely out of fear will have only one result - failure.

You see most people stumble upon their Wheelhouse by mere accident; they have no prior knowledge of it, nor do they attempt to seek it out in the first place. Once there they overact and feel that in order to escape this metaphorical prison, they need allow their emotions to consume them and burst forth like an out of control hurricane. This only tightens the reigns that bind you; the shackles that keep you prisoner. This is the purpose of the WheelHouse. What purpose am I talking about, youask? Well, I thought for sure you would have figured it out by now? The answer, my friends is freedom.

When entering the confines of the WheeHouse for the first time a person will soon discover both an alarming and amazing sensation. What is this sensation? Well, quite honestly most people feel suddenly trapped as if they are a prisoner inside their own mind. I'm sure I don't have to repeat the old adage that states, "People fear what they do not understand" so the initial sensation of fear is a valid one at that and should not be ridiculed by someone who has never undergone a transformation to such a degree as the one that occurs when inside the WheelHouse.

Patience is a virtue, as the saying goes. This phrase is truer for those people who shout and scream and hope to escape the WheelHouse before it is too late. You see, at first the WheelHouse will not be yours to control; such power will not obey your commands until you are deemed worthy. All you can do is wait for you mind to release you from the Wheelhouse; sometimes it can take hours or, even, days. Oddly enough many people will be strewn into a panic and will begin to frantically search desperately for an exit which in turn will do more harm than good.

Leaving the WheelHouse is far harder than you may first assume. Why? Well, just like any house, The WheelHouse has many doors and closets; some are locked while others are unlocked and seem inviting and serene. Yet, as time goes on this sensation of fear will subside and you will discover something far greater than you ever thought possible - everlasting peace and harmony. Once this new sensation overtakes you at last you will finally understand just how complex The Wheelhouse actually is. You will then know without knowing how to exit and enter this magical place at will.

But there is more to the Wheelhouse then just mere feelings.

Unbeknownst to many people there exist certain closets which are vital to our existence and must be opened periodically so that our soul can be replenished by joyful memories which heal us and give us solace in times of discord. Yet, there are also dark, foreboding hallways which seem to lead to nowhere with creepy closets scattered throughout the house. However, there is nothing to fear inside these closets; these dark, empty spaces are ones that we have yet fill; these life experiences have not yet happened. Therefore, we must be careful what, if anything we place inside.

If you allow your mind to escape the real world you will succumb to the fact that your WheelHouse connects your unconscious and subconscious to the reality which you chose to live in. In other words, think of reality in terms as you would, *The Matrix* but not a reality controlled by machines but rather by the power of your mind. It is this power that will connect you to the spirit realm; to a heavenly place. Yet, just like Neo you must learn to "unlock your mind and let go of the real" if you hope to truly grasp the power which the WheelHouse is capable of.

In today's society the majority of the world's population is programmed. We are told what to believe through the vast media outlets who tend to exaggerate (or even under exaggerate) world events, and sometimes fabricate the truth for the sake of a greater good...or so they claim. This brings me to my next point - there is only one truth. It may sound like an odd thing to say but truth is different for everyone. In order to discover the truth, you must go deep inside your WheelHouse to find the answer to a question that you never asked. But, how can you get an answer to a question if you don't know what to ask to in the first place? Keep reading this book and in time I will tell you...

PT. 3
THE HOW

Knowing how to build your WheelHouse is the first step in overcoming the challenges that you will inevitably face while experiencing what we, the human race calls, "life." Some people will construct their WheelHouse using standard 2x4 wooden beams and say that the walls are sturdy enough to survive even in the midst of a great storm. Others will use concrete and bricks and attempt build a fortress that would surely withstand the blast from a stick of dynamite. But, none of these things will survive the external forces that will attempt to weaken the integrity of your WheelHouse. I am speaking about people. Therefore, you must reinforce the walls of your WheelHouse with great strength; strength that you must create out of nothing and make into something no one has ever seen before.

   If you are patient and carefully construct your WheelHouse so that every possible weak point is securely fastened to an indestructible foundation, then your WheelHouse will become much more than just imaginary. In fact, you will surely see as I did that your WheelHouse will in fact become a shield that will encase your entire body and allow you to accomplish amazing things. You will have mental strength to such a degree that nothing can ever destroy you. You will conquer any obstacle and overcome any challenge no matter how impossible it may seem. However, just like any battle there will be "casualties of war" and overtime your WheelHouse will begin to crumble, and if you allow it to completely disintegrate into dust then you all you have fought for will be in vain.

PT. 4
THE WHERE

Where can you go when you feel like your back is to the wall and the world is against you? Your WheelHouse, of course! However, even while there the world outside still exists; time continues to move forward even though it [time] appears to stop altogether while inside the WheelHouse. As yourself - what would happen if you could live in two worlds simultaneously? Two worlds where time moved and stopped when you wanted it to? Sounds impossible, right? Or is it? You see what I have learned during the time I spent in my WheelHouse was that I was the creator; that I had the power to change things at will, and, even create new beginnings which I could make manifest in the real world should I want them bad enough. But, how did I do this, you ask?

It seems that perhaps I may have confused matters? Let me clarify. My WheelHouse didn't give me superhero powers where I could stop bullets like Neo from *The Matrix*. Still it did empower me. Though, not before I was confronted by some incredible hardships which tested my faith and brought me to the brink of insanity on more than one occasion. Each time I felt like giving up or worse jumping from a bridge I remembered that there was one place where I could go to to where nothing and no one could hurt me - my WheelHouse. It is important that you remember this as you continue to read the rest of this book. Why? Because I would bet money that you will at one point or another say, "If I were you, Drew I would have just ended it right there."

Everyone has a different opinion of what a WheelHouse is. There is no right or wrong. If your WheelHouse is a Bible, then who am I to tell you otherwise? Still, every WheelHouse gets its power from one single, solitary source (in my case it was two). This power can be whatever you wish it to be. It is this object of desire that is the all essential heart of the Wheelhouse and the one thing that can save you from a fate worse than death. It is the one thing that no one can ever take away from you, and the only thing that makes you who you are. It is your undying strength; your ultimate power which, if unleashed, will alter your life in ways you could never imagine.

BEHOLD THE WHEELHOUSE:
THE STRENGTH OF ONE IS THE POWER OF MILLIONS

You may be shocked to learn that every great leader such as Martin Luther King, Jr, Ghandi, Malcom X, John F. Kennedy, and, even the guy who runs your neighborhood watch all have a "wheelhouse." You may ask what is inside their wheelhouse? What are they hiding? What enables them to achieve such amazing feats that other men can never seem to accomplish? Though, if you are indeed asking such a s thing then you have it all backwards. Such questions are moot and used as a facade to simply conceal a much greater question; a much more profound secret. You see, I am willing revealed to you the secret of my wheelhouse. But, men such as Martin Luther King, Jr never did. We will never know what drove him to such ambitious beliefs that he alone could inspire change in a world which refused to change.

True strength is not apparent to those people who don't understand where strength comes from in the first place, or what the word strength symbolizes in the first place. There are many forms of "strength" as a matter of fact. However, many people assume that all they need to do is enhance their physic by building muscles to abnormal size; they trick their brain into believing that they can conquer anything or anyone as long as they have muscles the size of Massachusetts. As funny as it may sound even the strongest people who can surely be intimidating by their mere size cannot endure a two-hour session while getting a tattoo. They quiver, shake and complain about the annoying, and sometimes irritating sensation of the needle as it digs deeper and deeper into their skin.

Over the years I have gotten a total of eight tattoos which are scattered all over my body; each one a different color and size. I remember that on one occasion the tattoo artist (who was a close friend of mine) commented to me and said, "Damn, Drew, I know football players who jump from the chair and cry like a little baby. You're like a rock; motionless. You don't even twitch, for God's sake." I looked at him in confusion and replied, "Cry over this shit? They must be fuckin' pussy's?" He then asked me strangely, "Do you even feel it?" I smirked at him while saying, "Pain is only weakness leaving the body." He laughed and nodded his head. I then heard the buzzing of the needle continue and looked beside me to see blood run quickly down my shoulder. He glanced up at me but before he could speak, I blurted out and said, "Anyone who runs from a needle has no idea what real pain is."

Ask yourself: What kind of person am I? Do you run from a needle? Or do focus your mind and allow yourself to go to a place which is fortified by unbelievable strength; strength which is quite honestly beyond human understanding. A place I call, The WheelHouse? Do you see pain as a weakness? Or is your weakness pain? Do you simply turn off all feeling and become an indestructible machine? Are you human? Or are you more human then human? Still, the lingering question remains - Is it possible to truly achieve such a thing?

I used to be just like you and accept my limitations as a human being. That was until my two daughters, Sasha and Gabbie showed me that I could be something far greater than just flesh and bone. Like all those before me and all those who shall come after me I have only one mission; one destiny. I willingly walk in the footsteps of the past and confront challenges so great that other men would surely run from. I do this for one reason - to prove a point. You will ask, "What point would that be, Drew?" However, I am unable to answer your question. Why? Because that would mean that I have completed my mission; fulfilled my destiny, and as far as I can tell my mission, my story for that matter has only just begun…

PREFACE

Let me start by saying that this book is only the first of many books to come. After thinking long and hard about this book I came to conclude that I could never just write one book about Sasha and Gabbie (and my numerous other furry friends as well). While writing this book one afternoon and sweltering in the summer heat I realized that trying to squeeze so many special moments, memories and just plain common sense into a book that would be entertaining and informative would be impossible. Inevitably this series will go on until the day I feel satisfied with the story as a whole.

With that being said I want to mention that this book is not intended to make you cry though you most certainly will. This book is not meant to make you mad, however, it is inevitable that you will feel anger while reading certain chapters of this book. I am sure you already know why I wrote this book. If not then let me refresh your memory - to pay tribute to my dogs, Sasha and Gabbie; to keep them alive even after I am gone from this earth, and to enlighten those people who quite possibly the phrase, "They're only dogs." Though, my overall true purpose behind releasing this book is to show you how two of Gods most precious souls transformed my life in ways that the average person will never be able to relate to...unless you are a dog owner, that is.

Some of the events in this book are tragic (but not everything is as it seems). Yet, the real tragedy would be if I never had Sasha and Gabbie in the first place. Before they entered my life, I walked around unhappy and unwilling to smile; life had no meaning. In fact, I never understood the purpose of being alive? Many people may conclude (once completing this book) that I love my dogs more than a member of my own family, that I choose my dogs over a girlfriend (I am still single and unmarried so your assumption would probably be correct), maybe even alienate friends for the sake of my dogs well-being? Yet, these are hard questions for me to answer. Why? Well, in the simplest terms: it's a different kind of love between dog and dog owner.

It is a fact that human beings are incapable of unconditional love. Everyday love comes easy for anyone who walks on two legs, but unconditional love (and I do mean unconditional love) is a feat a human being can never honestly achieve. For a dog it comes naturally; in fact, it is inbred. For a dog it is all they care about. Human beings on the other hand care more about how high we can climb the corporate ladder, fancy cars, big houses, expensive jewelry, and, even, for the most coincided person, how many iPads they own. In other words, we, human beings, I mean live too impress friends and family alike, and even showboat to a random stranger. Love is something that we can do without as long as we have something else to takes its place. We do not need love to survive. We do not live to love and love to live. A dog on the other hand cannot live a fruitful life if it is unable to express the endless love it thrives on for survival.

Unlike human beings a dog does not know how to harbor hate and anger, animosity, jealousy or resentment. Well, no, that's not true. A dog learns to hate, to kill, and to destroy because its "master" teaches it to. Just like a child who is taught to hate, destroy or, even kill homosexual men and women, African Americans, Jews, or any other person (or thing) he or she will undoubtedly grow up knowing nothing more than what they were taught. The same can be applied to a dog's behavior. For me I taught my dogs to love everyone and everything they encountered even if that person or thing didn't show them love back. All it took was a day for even the most hardened person to admit that Sasha and Gabbie in fact melted their heart. Yet, as much as I taught them to love I also taught them to protect, to defend themselves, each other, their home and their pack. I taught them that not all things in this world are gentle and kind, even other dogs for that matter.

It was an incredible feat for me to train and discipline two dogs at the same time. However, by the grace of God I was able to do so. I remember that on more than one occasion people, even members of my own family would remark, "Anyone can raise a dog, try raising a child." It is true that a child cannot initially understand what its mother or father is telling it, however, a child in time will understand and comprehend language. Yet, a dog (or any animal for that matter) never can. Spoken language (and words) are beyond an animal's comprehension. Raising Sasha and Gabbie while trying to teach them right from wrong had to be done through body language. Try and teach your child to look both ways before crossing the street without using words. What do you think the outcome would be? Odds are you will fail at such a task. More than likely you would confuse the child and they would inadvertently misconstrue right from wrong and grow up to never fully understand the world around them.

Disciplining Sasha and Gabbie was difficult but I soon discovered that there seemed to be a "look" which made them lower their heads and put their tails between their legs. This look (along with an occasional smack on the butt or soft tap on the chin or nose) was all that was needed in order to express that they had done something bad; such as rummaging through the garbage, peeing in the house, knocking over my coffee from the table just because they wanted some, or even, at times snatching a slice of pizza from the pizza box I left on the kitchen counter.

It may be hard for some readers to believe but dogs do not stay dogs for long once you give them a "forever home" and accept them as a member of your family, or pack rather. In fact, a dog will inevitably take on human characteristics the more time it spends around humans. Take Sasha for example. In the early days she would sleep as any dog would; spread out on the bed lying on her back. But, over time something happened. She began to sleep like any human being would; her head on the pillow and tucked comfortably under the blanket. The truth is I never put her under the blanket or laid her down on a pillow. This was something she learned to do by watching me; by analyzing the way I slept. Many of my friends would often remark, "It's amazing how human your dogs are, Drew." I would reply, "What is a dog if not the embodiment of its owner?" I think that may be why when we lose our pet (or pets) we grieve harder for them than any human being. In some ways when our pet passes on we feel like we lost a part of ourselves; that a piece of our soul is suddenly missing.

Today I am grieving immensely while trying harder than I have ever tried before to tell you the story about my two dogs who have made my life complete. Though, I always knew there would come a day that they would no longer be with me I now see how wrong I truly was to deny the possibility of "life after death." My sudden change of heart will become obvious to you, the reader in due time. However, for now let me conclude by saying to all of you who have chosen to read this book - thank you. Though, I don't know you and you don't know me somehow, I feel that we have meet before. Maybe in some strange way we are connected to one another through our dogs, or animals even? I hope that your dogs (if you own any) do for you what my beloved Sasha and Gabbie have done for me and please tell your furry companions that I say hi ;)

INTRODUCTION I

I remember hearing a friend of mine say, "I loved your last book, Drew, but I want to know more about your dogs." I puffed on my cigarette and said into the phone, "It's funny you say that." I exhaled smoke then continued, "I'm working a book solely about them." I could sense she was smiling as she replied, "Good. I know how much they mean to you and it would be great to know their story too." I then said goodbye to her and hung up the phone and continued to smoke my cigarette allowing the ash to fall onto my jeans.

As the night progressed, I began to put more thought into the book that my friend was so eagerly anticipating (the book you are now reading). Though, I had mentioned I was "working" on the idea it seemed to fizzle out a few months later. I didn't stop writing the book because I lost interest in it but rather because many of the events that I intended to write about were emotionally draining. I was hesitant to think back to those days, to the times that I was confronted with questions, many which were seemingly unanswerable, and by fright so immense that each night I slept I waited for the inevitable. What am I talking about? Well, we'll get there. Though, first let me go on to remind you that not all bad things are intended to harm you, and not all bad events are meant to discourage you. Hmm, now where have I heard that before?

Within my lifetime (which hasn't been all that long) I have done much wrong; made many numerous mistakes and even counteracted those mistakes with more mistakes; some rash and others reckless. Yet, as I look back on it now, I see that these mistakes were not mistakes at all but life lessons that taught me one very important thing - compassion. I could sit here and list off the many mistakes I am referring to, but it would be a useless gesture. However, if there is anything at all that I learned from the experiences I have been forced to overcome it is that sometimes the simplest things in life are in fact our greatest strength.

Over the years I have written one book after another under the alias of Drew Evans (I've since retired that name indefinitely). In my previous books I have talked endlessly about following your dreams full circle no matter where they lead you and tried to inspire my readers with words of hope and encourage them to go forward even when they think they can't any longer. However, as many people have commented already it seems that, at times I was a bit cold and maybe even heartless. In some instances, my words may have come off brazen or even overzealous to some. The truth is those books were different. In fact, the circumstances for success were different as well.

This will probably be the only book that I will ever write that will truly showcase my compassionate side; my humanity. You see not long ago I was quoted as saying, "Drew is fed up with this world and the people we've become." Fed up? Maybe. Or maybe that's an exaggeration? Yet, the truth is that our society is blind. Our way of life is dictated by small green rectangular pieces of paper which determines our worth to our peers. In other words, the more money you have the more you matter in this world. Our similarities as people, as human beings, who are all connected to one another by the blood that courses through our veins is irrelevant.

I recall a wise man once said, "You can't take it with you." Those very words seem to have fallen on deaf ears. I say this because over the years I have had gut wrenching conversations with people who in my opinion seem to have their head up their ass when it comes to understanding the "meaning of life." Since the days of the Industrial Revolution our purpose as human beings has been and seemingly always will be - to become rich; to earn as much money as possible before we die. Maybe you missed the above quote? Regardless, it is a fact that no matter how much money you earn you cannot bring it with you when you die. You cannot clutch a duffel bag full of money in your arms as you enter the pearly white gates of Heaven, if such a thing exists at all? There are even those people who see not the value of money but rather fame and to me these people are the most dangerous of all.

You may ask me why? Why such desires for money and fame are dangerous? Simply put because they become what I call "false idols," messengers spewing forth a truth which they concocted to help further their own selfish ambitions. In the end it is their fame, their legacy that they wish to leave behind for their heirs so that their deeds while alive, their so called "importance" if you will be revered for all time and this in turn can and will secure an easy life for their bloodline because of who they are and where they come from. Still, such a relentless pursuit of riches or, even fame as a legacy will only ends with you, "The Pursuer" unhappy, and, sometimes, unfulfilled because you are existing and not living; for some remaining in someone's else shadow and none you will never escape; it is a fate you and your children and children's children are doomed to repeat. Such truths can be found throughout history in the form of parables form numerous biblical texts. Now that I think about it a very well-known and respected quote that will surely add merit to what I'm saying goes: "The sins of the father shall pass to the son…"

My conclusion to the age-old question of "what does it all mean?" is simple. In fact, it is so simple that it is very easy to overlook; misconstrue, if you will. What is it that I am talking about? Well, why don't you figure that out for yourself? Wait! No, that's wrong. What I meant to write is read this book and then and only then will you know without knowing what I am speaking of. That's not the answer you wanted, huh? The truth is that only by reading this tale (in its entirety) about two dogs who are so special, so unique can you ever truly understand my point. You see I could sit here and answer all the questions you may have about life, love, triumph and adversity. However, you would not understand a word I was saying...well, not yet, that is. Only by completing this book will you have the eyes to see what has been right in front of you all along.

As you will read in early parts of this book my dogs were nothing more than mere pets. In fact, I was just as ignorant as the next guy who thinks dogs are simply furry companions that keep my feet warm on a cold winter's night. But, then not long after something happened; something tragic but also something magical. It was this one event, this year long decent into the unknown that changed my life forever. For one entire year, night after night I felt fear; not for me but for her - Gabbie (my Golden Retriever). This was also the year that I opened my eyes to the world I thought I knew but quickly found out I knew absolutely nothing about. Since that time this world I cared so much for has become distant, alien almost, like the world of Terra from the video game *Final Fantasy*. I saw faces so empty, eyes so soulless and hearts so cold that my being, my soul seemed to change. I had to ask myself why? Why was I experiencing fear and sadness so great for a world I couldn't change? A sane person would think I was grieving over the loss of a loved one. Surprisingly, however the answer to that question was four years away, however.

As tragedy struck, I knew that I had help her, Gabbie, I mean. I knew that somehow I would have to make her stronger than she was before. I had to make her a dog that could do and be anything she wanted even if she did only have three legs. But such a feat would require me to sacrifice years of my life and willingly bankrupt myself in exchange for nothing more than mere love. As time went on, I would have to dive headfirst in the pits of Hell to rescue her (Gabbie), and as a matter of fact even trade places with her for a short while.

The beginning of this journey, however, would not start with Gabbie but rather it would start with me. I found myself in Orlando, Florida alone and homesick. I was relentlessly pursuing a dream, or so I thought. Yet, as the old saying goes, "Everything happens for a reason." My perception of what was happening and why was changing (as I previously stated). In time I began to find myself surrounded by weak people, people who needed help, my help to be specific. Regrettably, my first mistake was not listening to my instincts and walking away from these people. In some regard I have always been the type of individual who cares more for other people than himself, and that is where I have gotten myself into trouble. That mentality has more often than not jeopardized my livelihood and left me with emotional scars that will never heal. However, even with the tremendous pain I carry I know something many people don't. I hear you thinking, readying to ask and no I won't tell you what that "something" is...not yet.

Let me go back and remind you that Gabbie is not my only dog. As I mentioned I have two (as I am certain you have ascertained by this point?) Gabbie is a pure breed Golden Retriever, and Sasha is an American Boxer. Sasha was my "first born" and as some people may know Boxers are very hyper dogs and as puppies, they are almost impossible to train. Though, from the very beginning Sasha and I had a kinship; an unbreakable bond. I never thought I would say this but as funny as it sounds, I can recall the day I stood at the checkout counter at the pet store and asked, "How much is that doggie in window?" The price was nothing less than astronomical but as I turned to look back over my shoulder, I locked eyes with Sasha (who at the time didn't have a name only a number). I snapped my head back to the clerk and said, "I'll take her."

That afternoon as I walked back to my car with Sasha in my arms and a bag full of dog food squeezed between my ribcage, I felt like a dad who was taking his newborn child home from the hospital for the first time. The only difference between Sasha and an infant was that an infant could barely open its eyes while Sasha was excited and desperately trying to break the tight grip I had around her; she was overjoyed that she was finally "free." The only problem was that as she struggled against my grip (which she did manage to break free of) the bag of food suddenly fell from my arms and hit the concrete and spilled across the ground. Sasha stopped dead in her tracks and turned to me and sat down. She looked me up and down and seemed to be saying, "Well, you going to pick it up or what?" I could sense a thousand eyes on me, and I could hear ghostly voices whispering around me, "That poor guy. He has no idea what he's in for."

I left the food on the ground for the mean time and took Sasha to the car. I opened the back door and picked her up and gently put her on the seat. I closed the door and walked back to the bag of spilled food. Sasha was half in and half out of the car nearly dangling out of the window (which I left slightly open, so she didn't dehydrate or overheat). She barked hysterically for me though she seemed to be simultaneously mocking me. After I collected the food, I walked back to the car feeling like an idiot. I opened the driver's door and sat on the plush velvet seat. I adjusted the rear-view mirror and stared at Sasha who was panting heavily. I said, "Sash, me and you are gonna have to have a talk, ya hear?" She did nothing but smile back at me and all I could was laugh.

As the days and weeks passed, I knew I was in over my head. Sasha was a handful and often times I found myself shouting, crying out at her to behave, and all the while chasing her around the house with anger burning in my eyes. There were many times I felt like I made a mistake, that I just couldn't handle the responsibility of raising a dog. I muttered to myself, "Maybe I need an adult dog not a puppy?" Then the idea hit me that perhaps Sasha was lonely and just needed a playmate; another dog to keep her company while I was out at work? I shrugged my shoulders and thought, "*Why not?*"

As the thought of a second dog struck me like a lightning bolt, I suddenly felt a chill crawl down my back. At the time I paid it no attention and even now I am still unsure of whether the feeling was good or bad. But, if asked to give my opinion I would not hesitate to answer, "It was a good feeling after all." A day or so later I went back to the pet store where I adopted Sasha and asked if they had an older dog, one more docile than a Boxer? The clerk snapped his fingers and said, "I got the perfect dog for you!" He walked me over to a small window. I looked inside to see an angel resting its head on the sill of the plexi-glass. I asked the clerk, "How old?" He replied, "Twenty-four weeks."

A few moments went by until I felt compelled to reach forward and place my palm against the window and ask, "And what breed?" The clerk cleared his throat, "Golden." I furrowed my brow and asked rhetorically, "You mean Golden Retriever?" He quickly blurred out, "Yea." I stared into the window while saying with a smile on my face, "I always wanted a Golden Retriever." I then thought long and hard and rubbed my chin with on hand. After a moment or two I blurted out, asking, "And what about my other dog? You think they will they get along?" The clerk seemed distracted by another customer, "She's..." I interrupted him, "She?" I asked strangely. "Yea, is that a problem?" I bit my lower lip and thought about what to say next. After a few moments I continued, "I already have a female Boxer at home. Will two females get along, you think?" He smiled and said, "Well, you can bring the Boxer in and see how the two are with one another." I smiled and said joyfully, "Sounds like a plan."

As I walked out of the pet store to go home and get Sasha and bring her back to meet, The Golden (who I hoped would be her new sister) I asked the clerk, "She seems a little old to still be here?" The clerk then told me, "She was adopted once but the family didn't have time to take care for her. We didn't want to send her to a kennel; they would have put her on the "kill list." I pushed on the door while saying, "Oh, I see." I paused for moment then continued and said, "I'll be back soon. Thanks for the help."

As I would later come to learn there was a plan forming which was being concocted by an unknown force. How or why was yet to be seen. Though, as things progressed it became obvious that I never "chose" Sasha or Gabbie for that matter. In some strange way they were waiting for me; speaking to me telepathically and I never even knew it. I would even go as far to say that I was brought to Orlando, Florida for the simple purpose of adopting two dogs. Would it be crazy for me to assume that such a thing is possible? Well, now that I think about it maybe it's not so crazy after all.

INTRODUCTION II

It began like most bad things do - with a feeling of dread. I was on my way to Cleveland, Ohio to lecture at a film festival. But this wasn't the first time I would do so. From 2007 through 2012, I was invited by the Festival Director (and Founder) to speak to a group of Hollywood hopefuls about how to break into the stunt industry. In the summer of 2012, I decided to take a risk and move to Cleveland in order to take on a bigger role as a teacher and mentor. However, only three months after doing so I would realize that all I did was trade one Hell for another; in September of 2012 I would be back in New York living in a decrepit shit hole which I tolerated only because I had too.

It was sometime in the summer of 2007 and I was only a few days away from leaving for the festival.; this was the first year I would be attending, and my nerves were rattled; stress was something I could do without. Prior to leaving I began to get the sinking feeling that my trip was doomed from the start. I recall packing my bag and telling my girlfriend, "I'm worried about her." I knew she was unable to relate to what I was feeling as I listened to her continue and say, "I'm sure she will be alright. It's probably an infection." Looking back on it now I wonder if things would have been different if I decided not to go to Cleveland after all? I was only going to be gone for five days; however, I had a sinking feeling I was leaving her in the wrong hands. Oh, sorry. I forgot to tell you who "she" is. I'm speaking about Gabbie, of course.

To date I will never understand the selfishness I found myself confronted by that day. Of all the things I needed to help me feel confident about my trip it sure as Hell wasn't a soft, reassuring voice that reverberated in my ears which tried to convince me that everything would be alright. Instead what I needed was to know that I was doing the right thing by going to the festival and leaving Gabbie behind. I wanted to feel that I could rely on her for understanding and compassion; not for me but for Gabbie. Yet, that seemed to be an impossible wish.

It's hard for me to give you, the reader, insight into what happened to me that day. Yet, on the other hand it's not. You see for too long I was solely focused on me and my career (if you want to call it that). Girlfriends came and went, friendships ended, but, now, Gabbie needed me and I felt like I was abandoning her. This was an odd feeling. It wasn't natural for me to feel regret (it didn't happen often enough for me to notice I had any). Though, Gabbie was in pain. I knew it, my girlfriend knew it and so did

Gabbie. Strangely, moments later a feeling of immense pain overcome my entire body which seemed to be slowly paralyzing me like a Spider's venom. It was almost as if Gabbie's pain was my own. In a way I guess it was?

After I left for Cleveland it took me under an hour to call home and ask how was Gabbie doing? Then came the boom. "She's getting worse. She's starting to get aggressive," my girlfriend replied over the phone. I quickly blurted out and had momentarily forgotten that I was driving when I replied, "Okay. I'm calling the vet." A few seconds passed and the interior of the car was suddenly illuminated by oncoming headlights of another car which flashed a few times in my eyes; I was blinded but only for a short instant. I swerved the car back in the lane and asked, "Can you take her?" I sensed she was just trying to appease me; her words seemed cold and her voice was distant, "Okay. I'll see what I can do."

I was shocked by her callous behavior and immediately lashed out in anger and yelled into the phone, "Don't see, damn it! Do it!" She went silent for a moment. I then opened the glovebox (I can't recall what I was looking for) and my phone slipped from my neck. I could barely hear my girlfriend as she told me, "Okay. I'll talk to my mom." I exhaled a heavy breath and apologized for my outburst. I then told her, "If you have to carry her, do it. I would. Walk ten miles if you must, but don't leave her alone." Something told me she was angry though I wasn't sure why? Maybe I was being too harsh? Or maybe not harsh enough? She then asked me a question which strangely I found hard to answer, "Why are you acting like this?" Even though I thought of hanging up on her at that very moment I didn't. Though, it didn't take me long to reply, "Because I love her." I abruptly ended my conversation and continued to drive all the while concentrating on Gabbie; worrying endlessly about her. A few hours later I got a call from my girlfriends' mother who told me, "Gabbie's not doing well." I thought about turning back and heading home. I worried that Gabbie would be neglected or worse - be euthanized. I sensed that there was something terribly wrong and that there was no time to waste.

It wasn't long after I admitted my true feelings for Gabbie that my world got turned upside down and sideways. It began one day with my girlfriend who mocked my feelings and then out of anger told me, "You love these dogs more than me." To say I was enraged after hearing that comment would be an understatement. I looked at her with anger burning in my eyes and replied, "How dare you say that to me!" She curled her bottom lip and pouted. The realization of what she had said then took hold in her mind; she knew she had said the wrong thing to me at the wrong time. She was quick to apologize. "I'm sorry. I didn't mean that. It's just..." I interrupted her and yelled back, "Just what?!" I could tell she was thinking hard about what to say next; it was obvious she was choosing her words carefully. She then continued, "She's just a dog." What happened next was unexpected – I walked away. She called out to me, "Where are you going?" I said nothing in response and continued to walk furiously to to the door, "To get Gabbie. Where else?" I told her with anger in my voice.

I could tell she was watching me and expecting that I would turn back and give her a kiss before leaving to get Gabbie. I didn't. As I neared the front door, I asked her rhetorically, "You wanna know the truth, is that it?" I then paused and put on my jacket. I looked back over my shoulder and continued to say, "I do love my dogs more than you." She was shocked. Her voice pitched high at first then low. She replied, "That's a horrible thing to say!" I turned fully around and pointed to her, "No!" I yelled back at her. "What you said is a horrible thing to say." I took my car keys off the table by the front door and gritted my teeth then shouted at her in a ferocious voice, "She won't die, you hear me?" I paused waiting for some kind of reaction. However, she just stood there looking at me with a blank expression on her face. I then continued, "Whatever it takes!" I stared into her eyes hoping to see a glimpse of empathy then continued, "I will find a way!"

After a minute or two of annoying banter I saw her eyes swell and she was near crying as she replied, "I don't want her to die either." I looked at her and felt nothing; no empathy at all. I jiggled my car keys then put them in my jacket pocket. "You're a piece of shit!" I shouted to her as if she was a stranger on the street who attempted to steal my wallet. "I'm moving out and I'm taking Sasha and Gabbie with me." She gasped, "What?!" I reached into my pant pocket and took a cigarette form out of the pack which was slightly crushed and replied, "My father once told me that a good way to determine someone's character is by watching how they treat animals." She suddenly turned hostile as if I would be intimidated by her ranting and raving. She flailed her arms and shouted, "Gabbie is my dog! I gave you the money to buy her! You're not taking her!" I scowled and stared into her face. Then, almost instantly my vision turned red.

Sadly, I had no recollection what transpired next. In fact, all I could recall was waking the next morning in my bed lying half naked beside her as if nothing at all had occurred the night prior. Unbeknownst to me, however, I would soon find out that the battle was far from over. In the years that followed I would have no choice but to endure excruciating pain which in time would cripple me entirely. Still, as I cursed up into the Heavens shouting God's name and pleading with Him to come and rescue me, I then came to the sudden realization that there is no such thing as coincidence; no accidents, and, no mistakes. With this epiphany also came a life changing revelation - at last I had found my true purpose. Now, all I had to do was prove it!

"We long for an affection altogether ignorant of our faults. Heaven has accorded this to us in the uncritical canine attachment."

- George Eliot

CHAPTER ONE
BEFORE THE BEGINNING

Growing up I would often tell my mother, "When I'm older I'm gonna have two dogs and stay single as long as I can." More often than not she would respond to my statement with some kind of subliminal message, "Meet a nice girl first then think about getting pets." I would scoff and reply, "After the luck I've had with girls don't hold your breath." Yet, as time went on, I thought very little about what kind of dog (or dogs rather) I would eventually want to get. However, no matter how many times my mother would say, "Wouldn't you rather have a pretty wife and nice home?" I would rebuttal her question with, "I have an uncanny bond with animals, dogs specifically. Humans on the other hand don't understand me, nor do they try." I would then lower my eyes and continue, "And besides women seem to be few and far between." Our conversation became more like a debate which would last for hours. Finally, she would get fed up with my lame remarks and shout at me at me with frustration in her voice, "If you want a nice wife then don't dress like a bum!"

As the topic of the conversation shifted from me having two dogs to my attire, I did everything I could to attempt to excuse myself only to find that I was forced to stay until I agreed with her wholeheartedly. I would put my hands in my pant pockets, shrug my shoulders and tell her, "What you see is what you get. I won't pretend to be something I'm not; sometimes I'm an asshole and sometimes I'm not; I am what you make me." In some way she thought I was implying that I enjoyed conveying the appearance of a "bum" though in fact I was attempting to do just the opposite. Over the course of the next few minutes she would point at my Def Leppard shirt (which I wore religiously for years); it was half torn on one side just underneath the inner seam, and reply, "No nice girl wants to smell your armpit odor all day." I would roar with laughter and jokingly tell her, "Wait until she smells what comes out the other end." My mother would crunch her face, scold me and then angrily tell me, "Ugh! You're so vulgar sometimes." More often than not an awkward silence would overtake the air and I would watch as a few minutes later her anger would subside, and she would try desperately to hide her smile and conceal her laughter. Of course, she knew I was only kidding.

As the years past I found myself trying many new things, even jumping off of buildings for a living as a professional SAG stuntman. Years later while following my passion for stunts I found myself living in Orlando, Florida and working at Universal Studios performing as John Connor in the live action stunt show, Terminator 2 3:D: Battle Across Time. Prior to this I landed roles on national commercials such as, The John McEnore Show and small insignificant roles on blockbuster television shows like Law and Order: Criminal Intent, Rescue Me, and, even low-budget independent feature films such as, The Wannabe.

While in Florida I had my first taste of solitude and living alone in an apartment at the age of twenty-four was scary to say the least yet strangely satisfying. I knew I really didn't want to become emotionally attached to anyone at that stage of my life; there was still much I wanted to accomplish. Though life is unpredictable and soon enough I found myself living together with a girl who I had only meet two months prior. In the beginning the relationship seemed solid and even had the potential to lead to marriage. However, there was one problem (as she often called it) which was - Sasha.

Only a few weeks prior I had adopted Sasha and right from the get-go she was a handful. Due to her rambunctious behavior I convinced my girlfriend (at the time) that we needed to adopt another dog to keep Sasha company while we were gone. A few days later, we went to the pet store together and agreed to adopt a Golden Retriever who I later named, Gabbie. A few

already told

days later I would return to the pet store alone to pick up Gabbie and bring her to the vet for her mandatory shots. After the mandatory vet visit, I then brought Gabbie home and introduced her to Sasha.

From the very beginning the two enjoyed each other's company (Sasha and Gabbie, that is) and quickly bonded and became "sisters." Yet, I was becoming increasingly frustrated with the lack of commitment my girlfriend had; to her our dogs were secondary to everyone and everything else. I always found myself pleading for her to come with me to the dog park, play with them at home, and, even, arguing with her over whether or not "our" dogs could sleep with us in the bed. Over the years I became more and more distant to her and instead gave my love to the only two creatures who gave it back to me without contest - Sasha and Gabbie.

For nearly six years my girlfriend and I moved from one home to another. We both liked similar things; enjoyed rustic scenery and historic towns. As shocking as this may sound, I even helped her with relocating from Florida to Rhode Island and never even asked her for financial help. She worked her "dream" job while I made one sacrifice after another and put my career on hold. Slowly I came to realize that I had wasted half of a decade with her. I remember hoping against hope that she would one day become the person I thought she was. Sadly, that day never came. Like the old saying goes, "Nothing lasts forever." I am sure you can imagine that this so called "relationship" which I was trying hard to salvage with a girl I hoped to spend the rest of my life with was no different? In time I found myself conflicted, hurt, alone and depressed and I refused to waste any more time explaining to her why. Soon after my emotions would consume me and with the future turning bleak, I fell into a hole deeper than the Mariana Trench. And this, my friends is where my story begins...

PSALM 20

*May the Lord answer you when you are in distress;
may the name of the God of Jacob protect you.*

*May he send you help from the sanctuary and grant
you support from Zion.*

*May he remember all your sacrifices and accept your
burnt offerings.*

*May he give you the desire of your heart and make all
your plans succeed.*

*May we shout for joy over your victory and lift up our
banners in the name of our God. May the Lord grant
all your requests?*

*Now this I know: The Lord gives victory to his
anointed. He answers him from his heavenly
sanctuary with the victorious power of his right hand.*

*Some trust in chariots and some in horses, but we
trust in the name of the Lord our God.*

"The only creatures that are evolved enough to convey pure love are dogs and infants."

- Johnny Depp

CHAPTER TWO
BEGIN AT THE END

Welcome to the WheelHouse. It is here that you will discover the secrets of the universe, well, not really....

Hi there! My name is Drew. I have been authoring books for many years now; some fiction and others non-fiction. Before I bring you, the reader, back to the year 2005; to the beginning that is, I want to start this story in the present; in the year 2015. Some readers may feel as if I am writing the last page of this book first and first page last. Indeed, you would be right. However, for those that read this book in its entirety it would be incomprehensible if I did in fact structure the book in a normal fashion.

Let me begin my story in March of 2015. It was five days before my thirty-eighth birthday, and I was about to lose one of my best friends. Well, no, that's wrong. Let me call her what she is - my daughter. Over the years I have experienced death and grieved over the passing of a family member. This time, however, my grief would turn to something else (what exactly I didn't know). Though, as I sank deeper and deeper into depression and was overcome by regret and numerous other emotions which science has yet to name something wondrous occurred...she came back to me. Don't believe me? You will.

Now that you know how my story begins let me tell you how it ends. Perhaps I'm being presumptuous? Perhaps you have no idea how my story begins at all? Well, that's okay. In fact, the truth is that only by reading the end of my story first will you be able to comprehend the beginning. Let's begin, shall we? …

It had been nearly a month since Sasha first developed some kind of growth on her right femur. Initially the vet had given her some antibiotic and an aspirin of some sort to help the swelling go down. Still, I was panic stricken; unable to sleep and worried endlessly, and, even in denial that I may have to accept the reality that my worst fears may very well soon come to pass. It was snowing heavily, and the road conditions were worsening by the minute.

Earlier that morning I had asked my landlord (at the time) if he could drive me and Sasha to the animal hospital? He agreed and I immediately went upstairs and pet Sasha on her head and gently lifted her off the bed. I cradled her in my arms while walking carefully down the stairs. I spoke softly to her and said, "We're going to the doctor, Sash. Everything is going to be okay." I exited the house and approached the car. As I did, I saw my landlord sitting in the driver's seat. He unlocked the car door by flipping a switch from inside the car which was located on the driver's door. A few seconds later the door slid open on a metal track. Sasha and I entered the car and I gently placed her down on the back seat. I held her gently to keep her from falling over as carefully squeezed my body into the back seat of the car. I then sat down next to her; she could barely support her weight due to the crippling pain.

I recall the car skidded a few times and then swerved side to side; the tires were losing traction from the slippery snow covering the road. Sasha was trying hard to balance herself; she wanted to look out the window; she always loved watching the people and things as they sped by. A few moments later my landlord looked into the rear-view mirror and said while smiling, "Wow! Look at her. What a sweet dog." He turned slightly back and looked at me from over one shoulder and continued, saying, "She really loves you." I looked to Sasha and smiled then replied, "She's my baby." It was at that moment that Sasha laid her entire body up against me. However, her behavior was not normal, and fear began to overtake me. Though, as much as I worried, I tried desperately to keep my composure. A few moments later, Sasha laid up against me. I grabbed her tightly and pulled her close and began to play with her long floppy ears then kissed her wet nose a few times. I spit a few times and wiped my mouth with one hand and then said jokingly, "Ugh,

Sash. You got snot coming out your nose!" I laughed then pet her gently on the top of her head. After a few moments she fell forward and laid her head in my lap.

It was a short trip and took us only ten minutes to reach the vet's office. As we approached the building the car slid to a controlled stop and I eagerly opened the door. As I did, I was pelted in the face by large snowflakes. I then took a step out of the car and carefully picked up Sasha and placed her gently down on the ground next to me. Almost immediately she began to eat the fresh snow off the ground. Memories flooded my brain that reminded me of a time when we were living in Providence, Rhode Island when she eagerly anticipated snowstorms just so she could eat the fresh snow off the ground.

I held the leash loosely in my hand and took a step forward. I hadn't seen a small patch of ice on the ground and slipped and fell backwards and crashed to the ground. I quickly got and looked to Sasha; I thought that I may have accidentally pulled her off balance? I wiped snow off my pants and asked her, "You okay, baby girl?" I lead Sasha carefully across the street and entered the animal clinic. Sasha was excited to see other dogs sitting patiently in the waiting area. Even in her condition she still wanted to bully all the other dogs. I laughed and pet her on her back and told her to sit. After a minute or two she laid down and panted; the excitement was too much for her.

We waited for about twenty minutes until a nurse came out of the back. She called for Sasha and I got up while saying, "Okay, girl. That's us." We walked together down a short hallway which lead into the back into and entered an examination room…

By now I am sure you have already figured out what happened next? Sadly, I was still oblivious to the reality of the situation at the time; I refused to accept it. Though, as you can imagine this would be the last time, I would ever see my beloved daughter. I tend to think that if I only knew then that I would never hold her again, feel her pressed up against me in the middle of the night, or tug on her long floppy ears while we wrestled that perhaps I could have been better prepared for the grief which only days later would consume me like a whirlwind; grief that nearly destroyed me completely. Still, I wasn't prepared at all for what was going to happen next.

Numerous people have told me that grief takes many forms. They said that some people simply repress it; hide it from the world, if you will. Still, there are people like me who experience every facet which grief has to offer. For me every day was different. The grief came and went though over time the immense pain began to secretly dictate my daily routine. Then, without warning I succumbed to it and my life was thrown completely out of control. I remember telling my father, "When she was here, I never cried. No matter how hard things got I never let the Devil win."

At first, I was angry and, even, enraged. I felt that I had been cheated; that someone had stolen a piece of my soul and I was Hell-bent on getting it back. I blamed everyone and shunned anyone who told me to "get over it." Surprisingly, however, as people began to hear my story and experience my pain, they came to understand that Sasha is not just my "dog" but that she is my daughter. It was then that they finally accepted that even though she walked on four legs she was more human than they could ever had imagined...

My emotions consumed me as I walked out of the front door of the building and noticed that it had strangely stopped snowing. It was odd because only an hour earlier the streets were covered by fresh powder; I was certain the city was going to be blitzed by devastating winter storm and I would be secluded in my house for days. The sun was trying hard to push through the grey clouds and a blistering cold hit hard up against my skin.

I walked down a short ramp outside the animal clinic which lead to a busy sidewalk where people crowded one another. They were eagerly waiting for the light to change from red to green so they could cross to the other side. While standing there an eerie feeling came over me. It was a feeling which was similar to the beautiful morning of September 11, 2001 when I was abruptly woken up by my father who entered my room shouting, "Wake up! They bombed the towers again!"

I looked at the mass of people who blindly scurried across the concrete; many of who seemed distracted from the dangers lurking around them (such as speeding cars, ice and various other obstructions). All they could do was look down and press buttons on their cell phone or tablet. I was thankful that no one was paying attention me, however...at least not yet. It took only a few moments for my eyes to swell. I lowered my sunglasses and placed them on the bridge of my nose. I turned to the brick wall behind me and dropped my chin to my chest. My knees became weak and I fell gently forward and laid my forehead against the cold mortar of the dilapidated building. I whispered only two words, "Oh, God!" I then pressed my forehead into the brick of the building and scraped my flesh against the course texture of the wall. "No!" I shouted with all my might. I knew that by this time there were people watching me; staring at me, and, most likely looking at me as if I was an escaped convict hiding from the police. Seconds later, I broke down into tears. I stayed pressed against the wall as I tried to hide my face, but I couldn't.

The grief overcame me, and the sadness engulfed me. I took my cell phone from my jacket pocket and texted my father. "Sasha is at peace now," I told him. As I hit the send button, I could feel the breath be sucked from my lungs; I felt like I was suffocating. I then began to hyperventilate (but, no one around me noticed). An hour earlier I cradled Sasha in my arms telling her over and over again that I loved her. She laid still in my lap as I tried to balance our combined weight in the frail chair. The nurse knocked once then opened the door and apologized for disturbing me. I told her not to worry and she then handed me a box of Kleenex tissues (she knew I had been crying). I grabbed a tissue from the tissue box and the nurse then said, "The doctor will be in any moment." I told her thank you and then she left the room.

As I waited for the doctor to enter the room, I squeezed Sasha tighter and tighter; I refused to let her go. It was odd but it seemed as if she (Sasha) was more concerned about my health then her own. While holding her I pleaded with God not to take her. I asked God to take me as long as He gave me the one and only miracle, I ever truly needed for Him to perform. But, as expected there was no miracle.

A few moments later the doctor came in; her face was grim. I gently placed Sasha on the ground (she was happy and eager to meet the new people entering and exiting the room). The doctor then showed me an x-ray of her (Sasha's) right femur. As she began to explain to me what I was looking at my heart sank and I nearly fainted. I will never forget the last words the doctor said to me as I stood before her resisting the urge to cry. It was at that moment that I knew my life would never again be the same. "We have to consider the quality of life," she said. I turned slightly and looked to Sasha; she was waiting patiently on the floor. I then asked the doctor, "If you were me what would you do?" I don't know why I asked that question (her answer wouldn't influence my decision). I think it was just my way of delaying the inevitable.

The doctor waited patiently for my answer. While contemplating what to do I looked at the x-ray again and couldn't believe my eyes. It was an awful site. "So, what you're telling me is that the bone is completely gone?" I asked her rhetorically. "Yes," she replied while exhaling a long sigh. I turned my head trying to hide a tear as it rolled down my cheek. "And what kind of cancer is it again?" She took a pen from her jacket pocket and replied, "Osteosarcoma." She then turned to a folder with papers in it and began to write (I assumed about our conversation).

I stepped forward and looked closer into the horrible image protruding off the screen; in some odd way it was taunting me. I snarled and said into the beaming light coming out of the contraption which was securely holding the x-ray in place, "This is the second time you did this to me..." The doctor called to me in a motherly tone, "I'm so sorry. I know this is not what you wanted to hear." She then pointed to the x-ray and continued, "At best she has three to six months left. Maybe if we would have caught it earlier..." She stopped suddenly as I turned back to face her and placed both of my palms down onto of the cold surface of the examination table. I dropped my head and said softly, "Dear God..." I sniffled and wiped my nose with the cuff of my jacket. "My poor baby girl." I swallowed hard and my voice cracked as I said aloud, "I had no idea."

A few moments passed until I felt the doctor gently place her hand on my shoulder (I guess it was her way of trying to console me?) Though I appreciated her attempt at trying to cheer me up she had no idea of the amount of pain which was slowly overcoming me - no one did. She then picked up the folder from the table and placed it under her arm then walked to the door and said, "Just knock when you ready." I nodded and refused to let her see me cry. I paced back and forth in the small cramped room and occasionally wiped tears from my face. I was angry and with each passing moment my anger was increasing. I looked at Sasha and then kneeled down and held her by her jowls (I often tugged on her jowls when I would kiss her on her nose). Yet, this time I wouldn't kiss her. Rather, my body went limp and I fell backwards and threw my hands up to my face and cried hysterically.

As I sat on the floor crying, Sasha began to wag her tail; she must have thought I wanted to play? I sat there crying until she pushed her snout into my chest. I lowered my hands and grabbed her tight and placed her in my lap. I gritted my teeth and told her, "It's me you and Gabs forever, Sash. I love you!" I stood up and Sasha continued to wag her tail and jump around playfully. I walked back to the chair and sat back down and gently picked Sasha up and again placed her in my lap. She put her head over my shoulder as if she was whispering in my ear. All I could think about was if maybe everything I had just been told was a grand lie; a sick joke of some kind? Though, I soon snapped back into reality and admitted that what I just seen and heard was no joke, no horrible nightmare that I would wake up from at any moment. All I could do was reminisce about how I felt when I heard this same diagnosis nearly a decade prior concerning Gabbie...

In 2006, I found myself confronted by a heart wrenching decision. I had just returned from Cleveland, Ohio where I was lecturing at a film festival. A few days earlier, Gabbie was rushed to the vet where it was discovered she was suffering from cancer, Osteosarcoma to be exact. A few days earlier while I was in Cleveland, Ohio I insisted that my girlfriend find a way, any way to get Gabbie to the vet; even if it meant carrying her arms and walking miles.

Thankfully, she convinced her mother to bring Gabbie to the vet and look after her until I returned home. However, what I didn't know was that upon my return I would have to face one of the most difficult challenges of my life. It is a fact that more often than not I took on the responsibility of caring for Gabbie. As a matter of fact, I preferred it that way. There were few people (if any at all) that would give up a Friday night movie, Christmas Dinner or New Year's celebration and devote that time to ensure the well-being a "dog." More often than not I was forced to take matter into my own hands.

When I returned home very little was known about Gabbie's condition. I was fed up, so I decided to go the clinic and get answers - real answers, not bullshit theories and intelligent guesses. I remember entering the foyer of the clinic and waiting for the receptionist to hang up the phone before asking her to see the doctor. As you would assume the receptionist hung up the phone and greeted me with a warm smile. I told her that a few days earlier Gabbie had been admitted to the emergency room and has since been kept under a watchful eye for observation. Upon hearing what I had to say the girl's eyebrows lifted and her eyes widened. She said, "One-second, please..." She picked up the phone and pressed a few buttons and called over the loudspeaker for the doctor to come to the waiting room.

I took a seat by the window and anxiously waited for the doctor. After about ten minutes of grueling uncertainty the doctor finally arrived. He walked to me and shook my hand. However, I wasn't interested in formalities and quickly began to interrogate him about Gabbie's condition. His smile disappeared from his face as he said, "Follow me." We walked past the reception desk and into the back then entered a small examination room which smelled like rubbing alcohol. The doctor took a few minutes to arrange x-rays on an illuminated light board then a few moments later opened a folder and took out a short stack of papers and began to flip the pages over one page at a time.

I stood in the center of the room and listened as he told me the grim details. He explained to me that Gabbie had cancer and the likelihood of her surviving the surgery; that she may never adjust to be a three-legged dog. He even had the audacity to remark, "You need to let her go." I scowled at him then clenched my jaw tightly shut. A moment later I yelled back him, "Don't tell me what I should do!" He froze in place and stared at me like a child caught with their hand in the cookie jar. I then continued and said, "And don't you dare tell me she won't survive." I then pointed at him and snarled. "Who are you? God?" I asked sarcastically. To this day I recall how I imagined ripping his head off his shoulders with my bare hands; his remark was insulting, and I wouldn't allow him to verbally assault Gabbie regardless of the circumstances. Still, a small part of me felt that he in fact understood my sudden burst of anger but just didn't know how to convey that he cared. Regardless he had a shitty "bedside manner."

He quickly changed the subject and told me, "We can do the surgery and amputate her leg, but you have to know her recovery will be hard for her and you." I replied sternly, "I will do whatever I have to in order to help her; to make her stronger and keep her from ever knowing what happened and why." I'm not sure if he was mocking me or possibly even patronizing me when he let out a soft scoffing sound which I interpreted as some sort of sarcastic insult. He told me, "Dogs aren't aware enough to know about things like that." I lifted my eyes and looked up at him as a Cheetah would a Gazelle through tall grass as if I was going to pounce on him at any moment, and told him, "Trust me, dogs, as you call them, are more aware then you or me."

I told the doctor to perform the surgery and to keep me updated on Gabbie's status throughout the day. After he left the room, I picked up my cell phone and called my girlfriend and explained to her what was happening. "They're going to amputate her leg," I told her. She replied and asked, "How much will it cost?" I hesitated before answering; I wanted to scream at her but instead I contained my anger. I pretended as if I didn't hear her question and quickly blurted out, "The surgery will be done today. I am going to come tomorrow morning to be with her." Her voice began to *fizzle and crack; the connection was fading and then seconds later the call dropped.*

The next twelve hours were filled with immense fright. Every minute of every hour I feared the phone would ring and I would be told there were complications with the surgery. My girlfriend seemed untouched by the grave situation the two of us were now enduring. It was the "two" of us, right?" She went about her night as if nothing had happened. I remember sitting on the back porch; it was a quiet night with a multitude of stars glistening in the sky. A few minutes later she came out and sat down in the chair next to me. I was drinking a beer (which was a mistake because it was making me sleepy). She said nothing and was waiting for me to speak though I wouldn't, and a few moments passed until she began to cry.

A minute or two later she was overcome by spurts of shorts breaths (she wasn't hyperventilating but I think she wanted me to believe that she was). She then said, "I want her to be okay." I looked forward out into the darkness while telling her, "Cry all you want, but tears won't help her." I paused waiting for a reaction; instead she just stared at me. I turned to look at her and continued saying, "If you really care about her then come with me in the morning; show her that you love her." She sniffled and replied while she wiped her face with her hand, "But, I have to work." I sipped my beer and replied sternly, "So do I." She waited until she could catch her breath before telling me, "I can't just call in sick."

I got up from the chair and placed my beer on the patio table and took a cigarette from out of the pack that I had bought an hour earlier; I now had four cigarettes left. I left my beer on the table and light the cigarette as I walked to the sliding glass door. I looked back at her and shook my head in disgust. I then puffed on the cigarette while saying, "There will always be another job. But there is only one Gabbie..." I paused and flicked the ash off the tip of the cigarette and then continued, "And only one of me." She turned in her seat to face me then asked me with concern in her voice, "What do you mean - "only one of you?"" I exhaled a plume of smoke; somehow, I was able to hold back my anger. I rubbed out my cigarette in the ashtray then shook my head and looked at her and said, "You know exactly what I mean." It angered me that she was being coy, so I decided to go back inside and lay down on the bed. A few minutes later I was fast asleep (and most likely snoring loudly).

The next morning, I woke up to my phone ringing on the night table beside me. I glanced down at the phone and saw the caller I.D.; it was the animal hospital. At first, I couldn't pick up the phone. I hesitated more than once; I was dreading the diagnosis. Finally, I answered the phone. My girlfriend woke up to me talking loudly and rolled over to eavesdrop on the conversation. I heard the doctor say, "Gabbie is doing great!" A feeling of joy electrified my body. I felt like the world suddenly fell off my shoulders. "She is eating well and alert. Do you want to come and see her?" I was already out of bed by the time the doctor implied the question. "I'm already on my way," I said with excitement in my voice. I pulled my jeans over *my hips and began to look for my car keys (which I seem to misplace every morning).*

My girlfriend sat up and watched me search for me car keys; I passed by them more than once as if they were invisible. She pointed to the dresser and said, "Your keys are next to the T.V." I looked behind me and snatched the keys from the dresser. I stopped for a moment and locked eyes with her. "What are you doing?" I asked. She seemed confused by the question. "Lying in bed, of course!" She replied comically. "You think this shit is funny?!" I asked her without yelling. "Well? Are you coming or not?" She threw the blanket to the side and jumped to her feet. She grabbed a pair of pants then smiled at me and replied, "I'll meet you outside." I smiled back at her then walked to the bedroom door then stopped and turned back and told her," I'm glad to see you changed your mind." We locked eyes for a moment and I then heard her say, "Give me five minutes."

The faint humming sound of electricity could be heard reverberating off the walls around me; an eerie silence overtook the room and for a brief a moment I felt the presence of angels around me; I swear I felt a hand rest gently down upon my shoulder and it was at that moment I felt a calm; peaceful and serene course through my extremities. However, moment later the sensation of angels watching me would be gone and I would find myself once again sitting still in the chair pressed up into the corner of the room and holding Sasha in my arms; cuddling her as she laid motionless on my chest. It was then that I found myself begin to dwell heavily on everything the doctor had just told me. No matter how hard I tried I couldn't shake the image of the x-ray from my mind. Seconds later it hit me like a ton of bricks as I came to realize…Wait a minute! Let me go back in time to a year prior. This part is crucial part to my story…

In the spring of 2013, I was living in Kew Gardens, New York. It was sometime around three o'clock in the morning and the sound of cars followed by the occasional rumbling of a subway car reminded me I was still in New York (even though I often fantasied about being somewhere else). Somehow, I could still hear the road noise even though I was sleeping silently in my bed with Gabbie pressed up against me; it sounded like cars were racing through my bedroom.

Suddenly, I was awoken by an awful sound. I raised my head off my pillow and saw Sasha staring at me in the hallway by the front door to my apartment. She seemed in distress, so I called to her, but she did nothing but stare back at me. We locked eyes for a few moments until she walked out of sight and disappeared from view.

I sat up in my bed then wiped my face then rubbed my eyes. I cleared my throat and called for Sasha, "Sash, what ya ya doing, girl?" The hallway was eerily quiet; she didn't make a sound and I started to fear she was trying to rummage through the garage looking for my day-old Chinese food. I then shouted, "Sash! Come here!" Though, again she was silent. I threw the blanket to the foot of the bed and looked at Gabbie who was becoming increasingly agitated that I woke her up and refused to let her go back to sleep. I shook my head side to side and said, "Your sister is such a pain in the ass, Gabs." Gabbie rolled her eyes and stared up at me. She grunted then adjusted herself then shut her eyes and tried desperately to fall back asleep.

I got up from the bed and as I did Gabbie fell backwards and onto of my pillow. I pointed to the bed and told her, "Don't get too comfortable, Gab Gab, I am coming back." I then smiled and chuckled softly. Gabbie snorted and exhaled a heavy sigh. I told her that I loved her and then turned and walked out into the dark hallway. As I got nearer to the doorway, I reached next to me and searched for the light switch.

Without warning a loud bang echoed through the apartment; I had stubbed my toe on the corner of the entertainment unit which was barely visible since it was black and blended with the darkness almost perfectly. I reached down and grabbed my foot while jumped up and down on one foot. "Son of Bitch!" I shouted while rubbing my foot with both hands. "Sash, you are a pain in the..." As I spoke, I was suddenly interrupted by a disturbing sound. At first it sounded like she (Sasha) was dry heaving; maybe throwing up? I then felt my heart race, "Sasha?" I asked frantically. I raised my arms and held my hands out in front of me as I hurried forward through the doorway; I was protecting myself in case I accidentally ran headfirst into a wall. It hadn't occurred to me to turn on the light switch before walking into the hallway; I was overwhelmed with worry.

I got into the hallway and flicked on the light switch which was on the wall right outside the entrance to the kitchen. As the light illuminated the hallway, I saw Sasha sitting a few feet in front of me. I swallowed hard and then took a step forward to her. Almost instantly she got sick; throwing up and defecting blood from her anus all over the floor. I was strewn into a panic. I rushed back into the bedroom and picked up my phone. I then ran back into the hallway and kneeled down next to Sasha and tried everything I could think of to help her.

A few moments passed until I jumped to my feet and ran to my computer and immediately began to do a Google search for the nearest twenty-four emergency vet clinic (I didn't occur to me to just use my phone). It was hard to focus; my train of thought had become suddenly discombobulated. Within seconds I found one that was only three miles away. I dialed the number listed on Google and heard a woman answer. I quickly said, "My dog is sick. She's bleeding from her ass! What do I do?!" The woman on the other end of the phone didn't seem alarmed and told me to calm down. She then explained to me that it was most likely just severe constipation. I gulped then replied to her, "No, I don't think so." I looked to my side and hovered over Sasha; the bleeding from her anus had stopped and she was lying comfortably on the floor. I used one hand and gently pulled her up next to me; she yelped immediately. The woman on the phone heard the commotion and asked, "Is she in pain?" I replied without hesitation, "I don't know. Maybe I grabbed her too hard?"

I then saw Sasha paw at one side of her mouth. I said into the phone with fright in my voice, "She's doings something weird with her mouth." The woman then asked me to gently open Sasha's mouth and look at her teeth. "Look for any teeth that may seem cracked or dark colored," she told me. I exclaimed, "What the fuck does that have to do with..." She interrupted me and asked, "Are her gums bleeding?" I put the phone on speaker and then turned on the flashlight (on my phone) and used it to look inside Sasha's mouth. I said loudly, "No, but her breath is rancid." The smell made me gag.

The woman went silent for a moment then asked rhetorically, "She may have an infection or impacted tooth?" I let go of Sasha's jowls and sat down beside her and pet her gently on her back. "What does that mean?" I asked politely. The woman replied, "She may need to have a tooth pulled." I was growing agitated; I was more concerned with the blood coming from her anus then a tooth. "What about the blood?" I asked. The woman reassured me that it was nothing to be concerned about. "I'm sure she is just constipated. I recommend in the morning you call her regular doctor; they will probably prescribe a laxative."

I then began to relax and wiped the sweat from my forehead and asked, "And her teeth? Is there anything I can do?" The woman replied and told me to get a toothbrush and gently clean her teeth. I was surprised and replied curiously, "Seriously?" I then blew a kiss to Sasha who was panting heavily. I said into the phone, "I tried that, but she always eats the damn thing!" The woman laughed.

I told her I would do my best and she recommended that if I still had trouble, I should bring Sasha to see her regular doctor so they could sedate her and clean her teeth for me. I thanked the woman for all the help and then hung up and kissed Sasha on the top of her head and helped her into the bedroom. We got into the bedroom and I picked Sasha up and gently put her down on the bed. She began to relax and, of course, she laid down directly onto of my pillow; I was forced to pull the pillow out from under her so I could sleep comfortably. Though, Sasha did manage to take the pillow back while I sleep next to her. Gabbie, however, was slightly annoyed that Sasha was crowding the bed and used her body weight to cram Sasha up against the headboard (but, Sasha didn't seem to mind). I laid down on the bed and rolled over onto my stomach, and immediately felt Sasha plop her chin onto my back. I smiled and a few moments later I shut my eyes; the three of us fell asleep together.

I woke up the following morning and immediately brought Sasha to see her regular doctor. As expected, she was prescribed a laxative and surprisingly the doctor even gave me a free toothbrush and doggie toothpaste to go along with it. Sasha and I had returned home but I was exhausted from all the excitement the night prior. I decided to wait to brush her teeth; I needed a strong cup of coffee first. It was nearing noon when I decided to stop procrastinating and brush Sasha's teeth. As I began to brush her teeth she yelped and pulled away from me. I stood up and pointed at her with the toothbrush in hand and told her jokingly, "That's what you get for chewing on rocks!" I then pet her on the top of her head and told her to go lay on the bed and that I would finish brushing her teeth later that day.

At the time I wasn't too concerned by the abscess in her mouth. In fact, one day while playing catch with her in my living room she (Sasha) performed her own type of "dental surgery" by smashing her head into the wall and knocking the tooth completely out of her mouth. Whether she meant to do it or not I will never know? Amazingly, executing such a feat did nothing but give her a sore mouth for the next few days (but her breath still smelled as rancid as before). Thankfully, however, a week later she was back to her normal self and as eager as always to go for a walk; her breath smelled far better than a week prior. Still, I would periodically squeeze the sides of her mouth to see if she was hiding her pain; she neither whimpered nor cried out in pain so I was certain she was feeling much better.

A few days later it felt as if spring had finally arrived though the month of February had only just begun. I needed a pouch of tobacco (I stopped buying packs of cigarettes because they are too expensive in New York). I knew Sasha wanted to go for a walk, but it would take me close to an hour to get to and from the smoke shop; I always hated the thought of leaving Gabbie alone. Finally, I caved into Sasha as she *looked at me with her big, bright eyes. I walked over to the bed and pet Gabbie then said, "We'll be back soon, baby girl." She rolled over and looked at me then laid down completely on the bed. I felt that Gabbie was content with us leaving, however.*

I clipped the leash on to Sasha's collar and pointed at Gabbie and told her lovingly," I love you, Gabs. We'll be back soon," Instantly, I laughed as Gabbie exhaled a long breath as if she was saying, "Just leave already." I blew a kiss at Gabbie then opened the door and let Sasha out into the hallway; she nearly pulled me down the stairs from her excitement. I told Sasha to sit and then locked the bedroom door.

The sun was shining brightly as we began to head to the smoke shop. It was almost as if Sasha was more eager for cigarette then I was; she seemed to be leading the way. We strolled down the street with ease...that was until I heard a loud pop followed by a crack. I looked to my side and saw Sasha hit the concert face first. At first, I chuckled; she was a clumsy dog and did a lot of funny things. Though, as I would soon learn this was no laughing matter.

To this day I can still see her face; the look in her eyes; my actions that day are ones I will forever regret. It was as if she was telling me she needed help. Though, she never asked for help before; she was built like a tank. I wasn't used to Sasha asking for help in any way, shape or form. More often than not it was she who would help me; somehow, she instinctively knew when and how to help me. The truth of the matter is that most anyone would agree that she could bounce off walls like a rubber ball and never get hurt. Sasha was indestructible, or so I thought. Yet, I am sure you would agree that I was naive to think such a thing at all?

A few days passed until I began to see just how injured she really was. For the next few days I kept a close eye on her leg. Then one day it appeared - a massive growth which was the size of a softball. The strange part was that she never made a sound and all the while just continued to smile at me. I made every attempt to wrap her leg in ace bandages; even sedated her so I could put a cold compress on the wound. But, no matter how hard I tried her injury only worsened. Now, If I told you that I was afraid I would be lying. Fear (as it's called) is something I get when I ride a roller-coaster. The sensation that coursed through my entire body on that day is far beyond normal, everyday fear. In fact, I would later come to claim that, "Death was stalking me."

Sitting in the examination room I had finally accepted what I had to do. My heart sank with each breath and I told myself that even though I couldn't save Sasha from the cancer that was destroying her limbs I could at least stop the cancer from winning; from consuming her completely. I sat in the chair which was tucked comfortably in the corner of the room and cried endlessly. I held Sasha on my lap and squeezed her tightly and continuously kissed her on the top of head; I must have told her I loved her at least six dozen times within the span of three minutes. I said aloud though spoke softly; I was speaking to Sasha even though I knew she couldn't understand me, "No more suffering, Sash." A few moments later the nurse knocked softly on the door and entered the room. She apologized for disturbing me and placed a bowl of food on the floor for Sasha; Sasha jumped from my arms and devoured the food in only a few bites. The nurse then handed me a tissue and I blew my nose and stood up and the doctor then entered the room.

I was in a daze and barley even coherent as I heard the doctor tell me, "You're doing the right thing." I smiled and looked at Sasha who was wagging her tail and smiling and then replied, "I feel like I'm stuck in a horrible nightmare." I then turned to face the wall and covered my face with one hand; I was unable to contain my emotions. "Are you okay?" The doctor asked. "Mr. Glick?" I sniffled then cleared my throat. "I can't watch you do it." The doctor replied, "I understand." I sniffled again then tears burst out of my eyes. I overheard the doctor say, "You ready to go to sleep baby girl?" I looked at Sasha; I knew this would be the last time I would ever see her. I didn't want to leave her, but I had to. I walked forward and gently grabbed her by her jowls and looked deep into her eyes. I leaned forward and kissed her on her nose and said one last time, "I love you, Sash. I always will."

To this day I cringe every time I think about my actions that afternoon. Of all the things that happened that day; from the sudden realization that I was losing one of my daughters, to the urgent call I made to a friend where I told him the devastating news, the fear that nothing would ever be the same, were in minescule when compared to the look that Sasha gave as I left the room. It was almost as if her eyes were saying, "Are you okay? I'm worried about you, dad." I have tried repeatedly to make sense of it and even now I still can't forgive myself for abandoning her and allowing fear to get the better of me.

A few days after that horrible day a close friend of mine asked, "Drew, how you are holding up?" I replied, "Not good. But, thanks for asking." I tried to stay strong, but I knew I needed help (even though I didn't want to admit it). I went online and spent about an hour researching *Pet Bereavement Services*. Finally, I found what I was looking for. I sent off a quick email and made a few phone calls and a few weeks later I attended my first bereavement meeting. Before doing so, however, I tried to envision what the group would be like and what kind of people I would encounter? Admittedly, I was a bit nervous and even felt embarrassed that I was going in the first place; it didn't seem natural. I remember everything about that day from the moment I woke up to the moment I fell back asleep. It was a day I both loved and loathed…

The day was rainy and muggy, and the air was stale with a low fog that partially covered the top of the neighboring houses. I heard the wind howl and whistle through the window seams. A minute or two later, I felt strangely compelled to place day palm again the glass pane which was cold and covered with condensation. As I stood there a chill suddenly ran down my neck; it

felt as if the blood in my hand and arm had instantly froze solid.

As I prepared to leave and head to the train, I couldn't stop thinking about what I was going to say? Would I make a fool of myself? Would people think I was grieving too hard? Or perhaps not hard enough? It took me about twenty-five minutes to walk to the train station, and soon enough I arrived. I remember that I took my time as I headed up the stairs to the train platform. In a way I was stalling but something kept pushing me to walk up the stairs. I recall standing on the platform and noticed that there were only a few people whom were scattered around me (though none of them were close enough to me to strike up a conversation with).

While waiting for the train I light a cigarette to help calm my nerves. A cold wind hit my face and I felt small blisters begin form on my skin. My fingertips began to freeze, and I used the warmth of my cigarette to heat up my hands. I lowered my head to hide my face from the piercing cold and muttered softly, "You're not here, are you? Why would you be? This fucking New York after all!" At first, I didn't know who I was talking to but after a few moments it occurred to me that I was speaking to God. The question was could He hear me?

I took a drag on my cigarette which was now burning down to the filter, and then became suddenly saddened. I shut my eyes and envisioned a warm, serene place, and, even, Sasha running in a grassy field alongside Gabbie and I. "Lord," I said aloud. "I need to know. I need to know you can hear me. I need to know she's okay." A few seconds passed until I lifted my head and looked down the train tracks and watched the headlights of the train approach from off in the distance. "What a shit hole!" I stared into the headlights as they raced toward me. A few moments later I spit on the tracks and said, "I need to get the Hell outta here." I then took one last drag on my cigarette and tossed it the path of the on-coming train.

The train came to a screeching halt and moments later the doors opened. The electronic sounds of the train car keep me distracted from the endless array of individuals who seemed obsessed with pressing buttons on their phones and tablets as if they were programmed to do so. "Which one is the machine?" I thought to myself. "The phone or the person?" I grunted and then planked myself down in the nearest seat. I looked at the people around me in disgust and listened as the conductor began to list off the multiple stops that the train would make before finally arriving at my destination - Wantagh, New York. As the doors closed, I suddenly realized there was no turning back. Whether I liked it or not I was heading into the unknown; to a place where I had no idea what I would find, if anything at all.

The lights in the train car flickered on and off and then stayed steady for the remainder of the ride. I sat there uncontrollably bouncing my knee up and down while thinking endlessly about Sasha and Gabbie. I took my phone from out of my back pocket and pressed the power button. The screen light up and I looked at an image of Sasha which I added to my *home screen as the wallpaper. I remember I smiled but then my emotions overcame me, and I began to sob.*

A young girl around the age of sixteen happily walked past me and as she noticed me, she stopped and stared in my direction. She said nothing only lingered next to me as I tried to tuck my face between the wall and seat while wiping tears from my eyes. As I turned to look in her direction she was gone. At first, I was insulted but then quickly forgot that she even existed as my focus turned back to Sasha.

I then pressed the button on the side of my phone and again stared at the picture of Sasha. I ran my fingertips over it and said softly, "I love you, Sash," I sniffled one then continued. "I miss you." A few seconds later a loud screeching noise echoed through the train car and the conductor came over the loudspeaker. His voice was muffled, and his words were hard to distinguish but being a native New Yorker I knew exactly where I was, and how much longer I would have to endure the hellish train ride so listening to the conductor was irrelevant.

About twenty-five minutes later the conductor said (clearly this time), "Wantagh; this is Wantagh Station." I got up from seat and put my phone back in my back pants pocket and adjusted my coat. I shimmied through the isle and then walked out of the train and was immediately struck by a blistering cold wind that ripped through my jacket and nearly froze my skin instantly.

I then shook my head side to side and said softly but yet loud enough for someone next to me to hear, "I fucking hate this city..." I looked to one side as I spotted a middle-aged man who surprisingly stopped texting on his cell phone and stared at me in discontent. He quickly turned away from me as we locked eyes, however. I turned back to the stairwell and said loud enough so the gentlemen behind me could again hear what I was saying, "I'd rather live in Gomorra then this despicable fucking city..." I glanced back to look at the man. It was then that a single thought raced through my mind. "Why am I purposely trying to instigate a fight?" I told myself that now was not the time to start shit and I had to get my head "back in the game."

Yet, as if a voice in my head told me to do so I waited there hoping that the man would brazenly reply but he didn't. I then continued, "It's the people, not the city." I reached into my jacket pocket and took out my pack of cigarettes. I headed down the platform with an unlit cigarette dangling out of the corner of my mouth, and then hurried down the stairs and into the street. I quickly crossed the street scanning the nearby stores and buildings for a Dunkin Donuts or even, a 7-11. But, alas there was none close by. I pouted momentarily like a small child who was throwing a temper tantrum (I really wanted a hot coffee) then light my cigarette and continued up the street all the while trying to keep warm.

It took me about fifteen minutes to reach the location where the group was being held. As I entered through the front gate, I heard a loud boom echo in the skies above; a storm was close by. It didn't take long for the rain to start and for me to get soaking wet, of course. I growled like an animal then threw my arms out to my sides and said, "Why me, Lord?" I began to mumble all sorts of incoherent words (an array of profanity perhaps?) I then blurted out, "This is all I fucking need!" I anxiously looked around for a dry place to hide from the rain. Thankfully, there was a small alcove where I could keep dry and wait for the doors to the building to be unlocked; still it was freezing cold.

I stood in the cold trying to avoid the rain as much as possible. A few moments passed and I saw a car pull up and park in parking spot directly in front of me. The driver's door swung open and an older woman exited the car and quickly unfurled an umbrella. She closed the driver's door and then took notice of me and asked, "Can I help you with something?" I politely replied, "I'm here for the group." She looked at me in confusion and then asked rhetorically, "The bereavement group, you mean?" I smiled warmly. "Yes," I replied.

She approached the door and pulled on the door. "That's strange? It should be open," she said curiously. Almost immediately I saw a silhouette of a girl approach the door from inside of the building. I waved to the girl and determined that she was roughly around the age of twenty-five. She unlocked the door and introduced herself then allowed me in and showed me the conference room where the group was meeting. I listened and heard her say, "Everyone should be here shortly," she told me. I peeked inside the room and asked her, "Am I the first one here?" She nodded and replied, "Yes."

I shook off the water from my coat and then entered the room. I stood there watching as the young girl walked to the opposite end of the room to a door that was partially hidden by a makeshift wall. I called to her and asked, "Is it okay if I go back outside and have a cigarette while I wait?" She turned to me and replied, "Sure." I smiled and then left the room. As I exited the building, I saw a ray of sunshine burst through the grey clouds. I took the pack of cigarettes from my jacket pocket and placed a cigarette in my mouth. I cupped my hand around the lighter then struck it and took a long drag on the cigarette.

I stood there staring up into the clouds and looking at the only ray of sunshine I had seen in days. Suddenly, a voice called to me; it was one of group organizers. It was the woman who I met when I first arrived on the premises who had strangely disappeared after we entered the building. She introduced herself and I told her my name and then flicked my cigarette into the street and walked closer to her to shake her hand. We shook hands and then she said, "Follow me. We're about to get started." I followed her into the building and again entered the room; more people had arrived. I wondered how I had missed them enter the building at all and from what side did they do do? Did they come in another entrance that I was not aware of? Was there a secret entrance reserved only for members only? I sure felt that there was, and it was then that I wanted to leave more than ever but still I stayed because I had to.

I looked around the room and waited for instructions on what to do next? A few moments later someone handed me a clipboard and asked me to fill in my name, pet name, phone number and email. I sat in the closest seat and tried hard to write my information in a legible fashion. Yet, the blood in my *hands was nearly frozen solid. I tried over and over again to write but I couldn't even feel the pen touch the paper; my hands were numb. Eventually, my writing became scribble that appeared to have been written by an infant.*

I then got up and moved to a seat closer to the heater. Yet, to my dismay the heat wasn't all that strong. I thought about moving to another seat, however. I then glanced to the chairs and noticed that they were arranged in a broken circle, and there were at least a dozen people sitting around me in no particular order. I began to listen as each my fellow group members began to introduce themselves and why they had come to the group in the first place. I remained calm and collected and said nothing until it was my turn to speak. Periodically I rubbed my hands together and blew hot air into them to help warm up my skin. Then, my turn had arrived. I lowered my arms and rubbed my palms against my jeans to wipe off the sweat; I was nervous. I looked around the room while I told the people listening intently to my words my name. I began to go into a detailed description of Sasha (but, left out the bad stuff until the very end).

I remember being drawn to one person in-particular, however. I watched her wipe tears from her eyes with a Kleenex tissue. She seemed genuinely interested in what I had to say. However, that's not to say that everyone else wasn't. There was just an odd connection between her and I. I tried harder than I had ever tried before to not burst into hysterics as I began to tell the group about my final days with Sasha, and the excruciating pain I had felt ever since that horrible day. I then noticed that people's faces fell; their crooked smiles became frowns. Yet, somehow in telling about those awful moments I felt strangely better; healed in an odd way. Though, there was a part of me which felt that I may have inadvertently worsened their grief? Yet, I tried to remain confident that my story, though tragic in a sense would inspire people, nonetheless. When the group was over, I thanked everyone for listening to my story. As I began to leave, I was approached by the woman who I strangely felt connected to. She tapped me on the shoulder and asked, "Would you mind if I gave you a hug?" I smiled warmly and replied, "No problem."

I continued to attend the ground as often as possible. I let nothing stop me and traversed through snow, sleet, rain, and, even, intense heat during the spring and summer months. For while it was the only relief, I had from the pain that followed me around like a bad odor. However, it was what happened outside the group that really made an impact on my life. It was the friendship which I found with people who understood my pain; people who never dismissed my pain or the grief I was enduring which in time allowed me to rekindle the strength I thought I had lost forever; the strength which allowed me to see past my human limitations; to connect with my beloved, Sasha in a world far better than this one; a world where anything is possible. It was this one discovery that would save me from total annihilation and bring me back from an incredibly dark place which had me trapped in a state of limbo for months.

As time went on, I would unleash the strength that laid dormant inside me upon an unsuspecting world; taking them completely by surprise, showing society that love is the greatest weapon of all. However, it *is not* what I did with this "long lost strength" that is worth noting. Rather it was how this strength, or rather, my strength transcended through time and space to where it was later captured by numerous other people who then made it their own.

This great power, this unshakable strength is the legacy of my two daughters, Sasha and Gabbie. In fact, this is their gift to mankind, to humanity; a gift more powerful then you can possibly imagine!

"All his life he tried to be a good person. Many times, however, he failed. For after all, he was only human. He wasn't a dog."

- Charles M. Schulz

CHAPTER THREE
THE OTHER SIDE

What you are about to read may seem fabricated to some? Yet, I want to assure you that I am telling you the truth and nothing but the truth so help me God. I am precisely recounting numerous spiritual experiences just as they happened on that very day not so long ago. A small mined person will surely disregard these stories as mere fantasies concocted by my brain during a time of intense turmoil. Sadly, that is the reason why such a person will never experience "the other side"...well, not until they get there that is…

These are genuine stories in which I was visited by the spirit of loved one. Who do I mean? Sasha, of course! Whether people accept these stories as truth or maybe just a lucid dream, sleep paralysis or simply coincidence is of some sort is none of my concern. I know what is true and what is not. I believe with all my heart that I was in fact transported "somewhere else." I have not and will never question the authenticity of these experiences, and I consider it a privilege to have been given such a gift in the first place...Let's begin, shall we?

~~

Looking up into Heaven I saw her.
She called down to me and I heard her.
She walked past me, and I felt her.

It all began on my March 12, 2015; my birthday and one week to the day since Sasha traveled to a better place. The day started off incredibly hard. I cried uncontrollably from the moment I woke to the moment I walked out the front door of my house. For eleven years I have always had Sasha by side, especially on my birthday. This time, however, she wouldn't be there. Yet, sometime around 3pm that afternoon while I was at the corner grocery store getting coffee condiments, I would be overwhelmed by a force I can only call, "Divine."

It started simply enough - I left the house, closed the front gate and began to walk to the corner deli. I was wearing my sunglasses on my face even though there was no sun; it was a cold and cloudy day (I didn't want people to know I was crying). It didn't take me long to reach the end of the block where I entered the deli (on the corner) and walked into the center isle and began searching for Folders Coffee and some Half and

Half...and that's when it happened. The radio came on and a song I have not heard in almost two years rung out over the speakers. You're probably saying, "A song, Drew? Really? That's just coincidence." However, let me state the importance of this song before you jump to conclusions. You see, this song directly correlates to various moments when I had said the exact same words to Sasha and Gabbie. Let's see if you can figure out what I mean?

The song began at the chorus (which I found odd). I immediately stopped dead in my tracks as I heard the words echo around, "Don't worry child...Heaven has a plan for you." I became paralyzed by thoughts of Sasha and my emotions overcame me. I couldn't help but continuously think about when I had told Sasha, "God has plan for us, baby girl. We'll have to wait and see what waits in store for us." I stepped further into the isle and again began to cry uncontrollably. With short breaths I desperately attempted to hold back my tears. A few moments later, I placed my hand to mouth while tears flowed down my face. I asked aloud, softly saying, "Sasha? Is that you?" I could suddenly feel her
around me; I could sense she was trying to tell me something.

I regained my composure and paid for the items I needed then left the store and began to dwell heavily on why I heard that song, at that exact moment play just as I entered the store? It was too coincidental. Like the old saying goes, "There are no coincidences." A strong presence surrounded me which smelled and sounded like Sasha; there was no doubt in my mind that she was somehow still with me (maybe it was naive of me to think she wasn't in the first place?). I am positive that some people will certainly say that this experience was just a random act of the universe. But, would it still be random if I told you that later night, I went into Manhattan for the job interview for a lead video editor for a new reality show for YouTube...and booked it? Okay. Perhaps you're still saying, "I still don't see the connection, Drew." Well, here's where things got really interesting. You see, it just so happened that the name of the producer responsible for putting the show together in the first was, Sasho (the masculine form of, Sasha). You still think it was all coincidence?

Perhaps you still need convincing? That's fair. I'll continue by telling you about an experience that even today has me wondering if I had crossed over into another plain of existence? Sounds outrageous, I know. Yet, before you jump to conclusions hear me out. Here's what happened next...

~~

Our soul is shared by those we love. It is a vessel which allows us to communicate across worlds, through dimensions and within universes.

I can't recount the exact day my next encounter occurred only what transpired within the span of a few hours (at least I think it was a few hours). I spent much of the day in a state of depression, even intense sadness. I wasn't being productive so I figured I would lay down and take a nap; it was nearing 5:30pm. Sometime that evening I would be visited by a ghost, however. No, this isn't, A Christmas Carol, however, it sure felt that way.

As I slept, I was also awake. Maybe you've experienced this sensation? If not, then you're probably confused. In other words, I wasn't sleeping nor was I awake; I was somewhere in-between two worlds; I had somehow crossed over onto a plain of existence that is as real as this one. As I retell this story I would even go as far as to say that perhaps I was "pulled" over to a plain of existence far more majestic then any ever recorded in text or even holy scripture.

I don't recall much other than a few moments where I stood over my body (or maybe I was hovering) and watched myself as I laid on a pee stained mattress (which Sasha used as a toilet because she was too weak to urinate outside). As gross as this sounds, I wouldn't have had it any other way. Besides it wasn't as if this was the first time I had
slept in a bed Sasha had peed in. You'll understand what I mean in due time.

As I am sure you already know I was in my home sleeping; there wasn't one thing that was out of place or looked even slightly different. The walls were the same color, the television was where it would be on any given day, my computer was sitting on my desk in the exact corner that I put it in on the very day I moved in, the door and even the door jam was cracked in half as it would be in real life; nothing was any different than it would be if I was awake. Stranger still was how lucid the dream was and the realism that I felt. You may be scoffing at what you are reading but as I am sure you will soon agree - this was no dream.

Hours earlier I cried hysterically and laid in bed covering my face with one arm and hoping that my neighbors wouldn't hear my screams of anguish. I must have fallen asleep without even knowing it and that is when I found myself confused. I recall watching myself sleep. But, then suddenly the person watching me in the bed was no longer recognizable. The facial features had changed, and the air swirled in front of this strange figures face as to hide the being's real identity. I then heard the figure say in a deep bellowing voice which echoed around me, "Call to her. She knows you are here." Then, a flash of white light engulfed the room and I was alone. Yet, I could still feel a presence watching me.

As the looming sensation of being alone overcame me an immense fear electrified my entire body and my heart raced widely in my chest. I fought to wake up; punching and kicking with all my might; I was fighting against an invisible enemy and I was losing. I continued to struggle to wake up, and then without warning the room began to spin. I was becoming dizzy and felt nausea. Then, just as quickly as the room began to spin it stopped. I then felt weight in my lap and recall my arms wrapped around something or someone that was a few feet in front of me. I felt a tear form behind my eye, and I realized who was now sitting in my lap - it was Sasha.

You may find it hard to believe (at first, I did) but she was there, and my arms were wrapped tightly around her. I remember she lifted her paws and placed them over both of my shoulders as she did so many times before. She laid her head over my right shoulder as if she was whispering in my ear. I felt her cold nose press up against my cheek and heard her pant softly; her breath gently caressed my neck.

The world around then became calm and my fear slowly subsided. Sasha lifted her head off my shoulder and looked into my face. I stared into her eyes and smiled, and she smiled back, and then she was gone. My muscles relaxed and I was finally able to free myself from the paralysis I felt. I opened my eyes and look around the room. I called for Sasha. I sat upright and rubbed my eyes and felt my neck; my neck was warm. I spoke softly and said, "I love you, Sash."

To this day no one can convince me otherwise that this was only a dream. As a matter of fact, if you recall Ockham's Razor which states: If all things are equal then the simplest explanation is the right one then it would be true that this experience was a message of hope in some regard. Though, I'll let you be the judge. Ask yourself what you would think if such an experience happened to you? Perhaps it has and you don't even know it? Perhaps you've had such an experience and simply dismiss it as some kind of fabricated fantasy? However, dreams (if that was what it was) are an extension of the soul. Our dreams contain our deepest wishes and our darkest fears. With this being said could it not also be true that our dreams act as a gateway (or a door rather) to other worlds?

Having been exposed to this wondrous experience made me question the true power of the human mind. Over the years people have told me many possible uses for the untapped portions of the human brain which are still dormant today. It has been said that these unused areas of our brains may very well contain the answers we seek about the afterlife. Whether or not any of these theories are correct I can tell you one thing - there is nothing to fear. Life does go well after this one. Though, it may not be in the sense which we are accustomed there is a spirit realm nonetheless; an Astral plain where our loved ones wait for our arrival.

Some people claim that they can see this realm while others claim they can travel to and from it at will. Did you just scoff at my remark? I know you did. Don't deny it. I would have too if for not what I experienced. However, what I believe is that this realm is open for us to visit. It is obvious to me now that once we locate the key, we will find the door. Yet, for many of us this door will remain forever remain sealed. Why? Simply put - because the key you need to unlock it is hidden somewhere deep within your mind; waiting at that dormant part of your brain that you never use, and the only way to find it to believe that you can...

...Wait! I'm not done yet. There is one more experience I want you to read and pay close attention this time. Why? Because if you are as intuitive as I hope you are you will see that Sasha was all around

me and not just in my dreams but in broad daylight as
well...

~~

Our voice is carried by the winds too far off lands.
The winds speak to the trees and the trees to
speak to the rocks. Those we love listen to
the rocks as we tell the trees who tells
the rocks what we want our loved
ones to hear.

The day started off as usual. I woke and
cried...okay, well, that's not usual but it was quickly
becoming the normal thing to do after my morning
coffee. I knew that on this day I had to keep my shit
together. I had an important film shoot and couldn't let
my co-workers feel as if I was distant or uninterested.

Prior to this day I began to notice a strange
series of events which occurred each time I passed a
random dog on the street. More often than not the dog,
well, every dog for that matter would briefly lock eyes
with me then pull its "master" in my direction, and then
stop and stare at me for a few seconds. When this
would happen, the dog would sniff me, and I would
exchange a few words with the owner who always
apologized for the dog's behavior. I would hear, "Sorry,
sir. My dog is usually not this friendly..." and, of course
I would nod and say, "No problem."

Now, this isn't the strange part about this
story...I'll get right to the point. As we began to shoot a
massive King German Shepard (which was off the

leash) trotted at a steady pace in my direction. I was holding the camera and didn't notice the beast until the very last second. However, the actors were strangely standing still. I lowered the camera slightly and before I could speak, I saw the massive Shepard dash over to me. However, it ignored the three actors standing directly in front of me and seemed only interested in me.

A few moments later the same thing which had occurred prior happened again - the dog sniffed me and then left in peace. I looked up at one of the actors as I heard him say, "Shit, Drew! I thought you were about to get bite." I chuckled but didn't reveal why I was unafraid. I knew he would think I was crazy if I told him that this wasn't the first time a dog had stopped to smell me.

Let me just say that until the day Sasha passed on, I was never approached by a random dog in such a fashion. These unexpected "meetings" with such lovable dogs made me aware that Sasha was speaking to me in a way that only I could understand. In some odd way she was commanding these dogs to simply say "hi."

Following that day these meetings occurred over and over again. Though, I was always overjoyed when they did, I was saddened as the film project I was working on fell apart. It did so because I was unable to come to place of peace and confront in my mind and heart. I tried hard to follow through on my commitments, but life was becoming harder and harder with each passing moment. I had to make a decision

and determine what was in my best interest? Should I stay or should I go? A few weeks later I
began to withdraw from society and make up excuses and, even, lie to cover up the emotional trauma I was enduring. I couldn't bear thought of being seen as weak. So, I simply became a hermit.

Prior to the project falling to pieces, however, we were successful with releasing a forty-minute short to IMDb.com. No matter what happened following the release of the short I was glad to have had the opportunity to showcase the film's true potential to film buffs everywhere.

"I think dogs are the most amazing creatures;
they give unconditional love. For me they are the
role model for being alive."

- Gilda Radner

CHAPTER FOUR
ANGELS IN DISGUISE

Someone once told me, "Be careful how you treat a stranger. He (or she) could be an Angel is disguise." I guess such a quote would seem outlandish to some people. Yet, for me on the other hand I had only one single thought that coursed through my brain as I remembered the saying years later. "Do Angels only come in human form?" On numerous occasions I attempted to see through people as I passed them on the street. I will admit that at times I looked for a bulge on their back underneath their jacket hoping to see a glimpse of white wings. Though, as this process of unmasking a "real" angel faded out of my mind there were still moments when I wondered if such a thing was possible - to see an Angel. The fact was that I was already living with two angels who clinged to me like velcro. However, it would take years for me to realize it.

As a matter of fact, the day I discovered the presence of two Angels right in my own living room was the day I opened up my mind to the possibility of divine intervention. Yet, to my surprise there were no white wings, no halo circling the head, only fur, floppy ears and drool that covered every inch of my sofa. Yet, these two angels seemed, at times, like little Devils who tested my patience on more than one occasion...

FOLLOW YOUR PATH

Sometimes (maybe more often then we know) angels come into our lives for an array of reasons; sometimes to help us and other times seeking our help. In this particular instance two angels called out to me from a far seeking my help. Whether I spoke to them on a subconscious level or acted on instinct I answered their call because no one else would. What they gave me in return was beyond my wildest dreams. Of course, I won't spoil it for you. What would be the purpose of reading this book if I did? However, then again, I think I may already have.

Let me start this part of the book by telling you that I had just moved to Orlando, Florida; I had relocated there to pursue a job. But, the reality of the situation became clear when one day I said, "I want a dog." Years later I would put the pieces together and come to realize that my move to Florida had many purposes; many of them far greater than just a job. In fact, the most important reason above all others would undoubtedly be - Sasha and Gabbie.

It was sometime in June of 2004 when I first went to the pet store and looked through the glass window and watched as puppies of all different breeds (no bigger than the size of my hand) scurried around a small enclosure; running and playing with one another. I knew I wanted a dog who looked mean but was gentle, sweet and loving. I wasn't too familiar with "Boxers," however. In fact, I mistakenly identified them as a cross breed between a Bulldog and a Pit bull. For years I heard horror stories about Pit bulls and how they can suddenly turn from docile to aggressive in the blink of an eye, and even confused a Pitfall and Boxer due to the striking similarities. Yet, the more I watched the Boxer puppies play amongst themselves (and came to realize they were not related to Pitbull's) the more I realized that there wasn't a mean bone in their body.

Off in the corner was a sole Boxer pup (no more than a few weeks old). I looked at her (at least I thought it was a her) and waved hello. Her long floppy ears covered her eyes; they were bigger than her face. She was curled up in a fetal position with her short snout tucked under her belly. I tapped gently on the window and her eyes sprung open. She looked at me as if she was angry for waking her up. She seemed to snarl (but, it was cute snarl). I watched her with a smile streaking across my face and softly whispered, "Hey, Sasha." I don't know why I called her "Sasha" but the name seemed to fit her perfectly.

After I called to her through the window she jumped up (stumbling once but quickly regaining her balance). She stood before me looking at me as if to say, "Okay. I'm up. Now what?" Her tongue was hanging down and she was panting; she appeared happy. I felt a hand touch my shoulder; it was young man who worked at the pet store. He spoke softly and his voice was friendly. I listened as he said, "She seems to like you." I turned slightly and looked back at him and replied, "The feeling is mutual." He moved in front of me and took a set of keys from his pocket and asked, "Would you like to see her? Play with her, I mean?" I nodded and stepped back so I wouldn't be in his way. He fumbled with the lock as he told me, "Go back to the play pen," he pointed past me and continued, "The one over there and I'll bring her to you in a few minutes." I placed my palm on the glass where "the Boxer" eagerly waited to be taken out.

I sat in the "play pen" wiping the sweat from my hands onto my jeans as I waited patiently. A few minutes later I could see the young man walking down the aisle cradling "Sasha" in his arms as if she was an infant child. "Sasha" seemed calm but seemed to be inspecting her surroundings very carefully, however. The young man opened the swinging barn door to the play pen and gently placed "Sasha" on the floor. "Sasha" sat down at my feet and looked up at me. I leaned forward and reached for her; she jerked away and ran back to the young man (who she cowered behind and sought protection). The young man told me it was normal for a newborn pup to be cautious of new things (and sometimes people) which they didn't understand. He gave me a treat to give to "Sasha"; a small horrible smelling cookie that smelled more like rotten food than a "treat."

I held the treat in front of me and coxed Sasha, I mean "The Boxer" to come to me (by now I think you get my point?) Let's just call her, Sasha from here on forward, shall we? Sasha slowly inched closer and closer to me all the while sniffing the air in front of her; I guess she was trying to determine if the "treat" was something she would enjoy eating? In a quick motion she snatched the treat from my hand, and I jerked away. "Wow!" I exclaimed. "She's got some spunk in her, doesn't she?" I said with a chuckle. The young man replied, "Well, she is a Boxer." We laughed in unison.

From seemingly out of nowhere Sasha let out an earth-shattering howl. The sound reverberated around me; her howl scared me, and my body jerked as if I had just been jolted with a static shock. A few seconds later, Sasha barked, then barked again and again. I asked the young man, "Is she scared of me?" He bent down and pet Sasha on her back then patted her softly on her rear end and said, "No. Actually, that's her way of saying she likes you."

I knew there was a lot I had to learn about raising a dog. First and foremost, I had to learn about responsibility. Even at that moment in time which I call "love at first sight" I had yet to comprehend the challenges that awaited me. Deep down in the bowels of my soul I heard myself asking if I could actually succeed? I wondered if I had what it took to sacrifice years of my life for the life of another? Could I truly devote myself to the well-being of a dog? (No matter how cute she was). In a way I was asking myself what, if anything I was capable of? I didn't want to admit it, but I felt inferior to all the other dog owners out there who have successfully raised a puppy into adulthood. Though, in a strange way I already knew that no matter what happened; good or bad, me and Sasha were "two pea's in a pod." Still, I felt something was missing. That our pack was incomplete.

Initially, I thought I needed a girlfriend; someone to keep Sasha company while I was at work who would love her just as much as I did. Though, as I'm sure you can imagine that's easier said than done. However, only a few short weeks later I would make drastic changes to my lifestyle that would both shock and amaze my family and friends. As a matter of fact, I would shock myself just as much as I did anyone else (possibly even more so). This is where I would not only become involved a six-year relationship that had the potential to lead to marriage (but, ended in disaster). Yet, I would find out what I was doing here in the first place. Orlando, I mean.

A DAY IN THE LIFE OF SASHA
BABY BOXERS ARE ADORABLE UNTIL....

While in Orlando, Florida I found it hard to relate to people. In fact, New Yorkers often have a hard time relating to anyone who is not native to "The Big Apple." But thankfully I had an advantage. I had lived all over the country, visited many foreign lands, and made friends with many interesting people.

I will never forget the day I arrived in Orlando. I had been driving for nearly twenty-four hours straight with very little to eat and only coffee and cigarettes to help stimulate my brain with the hopes of keeping my motor functions active and alert. Before moving my stuff into my new apartment, I decided I would go to a McDonald's and get something to eat. I recall coming to a slow stop at the drive through and hearing a male voice ask me, "How y'all doing today?" I paused for a moment when I finally realized I was now in the south and would have to tolerate the horrendous accent that always started or ended with the word, "Y'all." I placed my left arm on the windowsill and leaned out the driver's side window and then replied, "Yea, can I get a..." Within seconds the male voice came over the speaker and interrupted me and said, "Go home, Yankee!" I was shocked. I slightly opened the driver's doors and stood halfway out while asking with an aggressive tone, "What the fuck did you just say?" The man said nothing, so I asked again. "Yo!" I shouted into the intercom. "You gonna answer me or what?" Still, there was no response.

I sat back down in the driver's seat and slammed the door closed and stomped own the gas pedal and burned the rubber of the tires and sped up to the drive through window. As I got there, I saw a male heavy-set teenager staring me through the glass like a deer caught in the headlights of an oncoming car. He swallowed hard and hesitated to come to the window. I sat there inconspicuously while bouncing my left knee uncontrollably. After a few minutes the heavy-set teenager finally came to the window and opened it slightly. He peered out at me keeping a safe distance just in case I lunged at him. I did nothing but stare into his face.

After a minute or two a car horn honked loudly behind me. I looked in the rear-view mirror and signaled to the driver I wouldn't be much longer. I then took a cigarette out of the pack that was lying still in the console and placed it in my mouth. I glanced over to the window and looked at the worker on the other side of the window and then turned back and light the cigarette dangling from my lips. I inhaled deeply then blew a heavy plume of smoke out of my mouth and through the small drove through window and into the building. I then revved the engine of the car and watched as the teenager who brazenly insulted me was pushed aside by an older woman (probably the manager of the establishment). She apologized for the man's comment and then handed me a brown bag full of French fires and cheeseburgers. I looked at her and shook my head and said, "Keep it. He probably spit in it." The woman then assured me the burgers were free of any human fluids. I thought for a moment and then snatched the bag from her hand; my hunger was insatiable.

I secured the bag of food in the seat next to me. I then looked back at the woman while saying, "Do me a favor," I then paused and reached into the brown bag and chomping on French fries. I then continued, "Remind that dimwit that the North won." I then sped away leaving tire treads and chocking white smoke behind me. I sped down the street swearing around traffic; I was anxious to get to my new apartment. While driving recklessly I tried hard to forget about the confrontation I just had with an uneducated imbecile. After a few minutes I called my nerves and smiled happily as I pulled into the culdesac of my new apartment complex.

I arrived at the leasing office and quickly jumped from the car and walked into the cool air-conditioned foyer. I looked to my side and saw a young girl sitting her desk and writing in a notebook. She didn't notice me as I entered. I was a bit nervous that my sudden presence would startle her so rather than call out to her I gently cleared my throat. She lifted her head almost instantly and greeted me with a smile. She got up from her desk and held her arm out in front of her. "You must be Andrew?" She asked. I wiped my brow with one hand and replied, "Call me, Drew." She shook my hand and lead me into her office.

As I entered the office, I pulled a chair from under the desk and sat down. She asked me to wait while she went to get my lease and keys. I nodded my head and patiently waited for her return. After a few minutes she returned with a large stack of papers and a set of silver keys. She laid the papers down on the desk before me and said, "This is your lease. Take a moment to read it if you like." She placed a ball point pen down in front of me and said, "When you finished just sign where the highlighted sections and I'll give you the keys." I thumbed through the pages of the lease while twiddling the pen in my opposite hand. I eagerly signed each section and when done handed the lease back to her and said, "Here ya go! All finished." She took the lease and double checked it then stood up and handed me the door keys. She smiled while saying, "Welcome home."

She opened the door to the office and asked me if I need her help in finding the correct apartment? I told her that I would be fine and was eager to get some sleep. She shook my hand and wished me good luck and then closed the office door behind me. I walked back to my car and noticed a few of the residents were walking their dogs. I smiled and waved to each of them; they waved back and greeted me with a warm "hello."

I hurried to my new apartment and began to immediately take boxes from the truck of the car and rush them upstairs. I remember placing the last of the boxes on the floor and immediately turning the television on. Sadly, I had no furniture; most of it was scheduled to be delivered later in the week. I placed my blanket on the floor to help create more cushion on the hard floor and then rested the pillow against the wall. I laid down and moments and hit play on the DVD player; I believe I was watching Empire Strikes Back but I can't be sure. I then propped myself up on the pillow and sat against the wall. Suddenly, I heard dogs begin to bark widely outside.

I grunted and then got up off the floor and looked out the window. I shielded my eyes from the sun scorching sun with one hand as I pressed my forehead up against the glass patio door and looked across to the adjacent building. I saw two puppies of different breeds playing with one another while occasionally chasing around a tennis ball. I watched the puppies play for a minute or two then went back to my makeshift bed where I was overcome by swooshing lightsaber sounds and blaster fire. I sat back down, and this time snuggled under the blanket and rested my head on the pillow and moments later became mesmerized in the lightsaber duels erupting on the television screen. I remember I had only a single thought course through my mind as I drifted off in La La Land. My brain wandered as I thought, "I wonder what it would be like to have a dog?"

I wasn't scheduled to begin work for another two days so I decided to scope out the town and get a bearing. I discovered that directly across from me was a mall with Walmart and other well-known store chains. However, I would frequently visit only two stores in-particular. The first was, GameStop where I would periodically go get new titles for my PlayStation and Xbox. The second was, yup, you guessed - the pet store. Following the weekend, I began my training for my new role as, *John Connor* in *Terminator 2 3D: Battle Across Time Live Action Stunt Show.*

While training I didn't think much about my next visit to the pet store or the upcoming releases for PlayStation for that matter (back then like any guy I was an avid gamer). Yet, instead like all guys I was thinking about money and women and even more so now that I was in Florida where bikinis were an everyday thing. At my job there where many attractive girls, excuse me, Young Ladies who were near or close to my age but the really good-looking ones were older than me, and often times I was caught staring but can you blame me. I mean after I was still young and stupid. Though, even though I thought about dating I was still hesitant because I was weary about whether or not I would stay in Orlando. I surely didn't want to get stuck in an uncomfortable situation or ugly break up.

To this day I still don't know who approached who but somehow, I found myself attending a Nine Inch Nails concert with a girl who adamantly denied to her friends that she had no romantic interest in me whatsoever. After the concert we began seeing each other more frequently and not just at work. We went to each other's house and even stayed over one another's place from time to time. I was only living in Florida for a little under three months when I got a phone call from my father who said, "We're coming to see you." I was shocked and replied, "Who's we?" My father shuffled the phone and happily said, "Me and mom, well, the whole family!" I wiped my face with one hand and told him, "Are you serious?" He chuckled and replied, "Yup!" I sat down on the couch which had arrived about three days prior and said, "I should probably tell you something before you come, dad." He seemed to be scolding me as he replied, "You got fired already!" I knew he was kidding but I replied, insisting, "No, I didn't get fired." I then cleared my throat and continued, "I got a dog."

He went silent for a moment or two then told me, "Bring the dog back. You can't handle a pet right now. Trust me..." I interrupted him, "Stop it, dad." I sighed. "I'm not bringing Sasha back." He seemed surprised and asked, "Sasha?" I replied quickly, "Yea, that's what I named her." He seemed intrigued, "Sasha, huh? Interesting name." I stood up and looked at Sasha who was sleeping peacefully in her crate. I then listened as he asked me, "What kind of dog is she?" I kneeled down and unlocked the crate door then reached inside and pet Sasha gently on the top of her head. I stood tall and replied, "A Boxer." He shuffled the phone again and replied, "Well, I can't wait to meet her - Sasha." After my father and I hung up I gently took Sasha out of her crate and let her freely roam around the apartment. I was hoping that the crate would help her to become house trained? After a few weeks, however, it turned out that the crate was nothing more than a waste of money. A few weeks later I ended up giving it away to neighbor.

Before my family arrived in Orlando, Florida I did everything I could to try and get Sasha house trained. I knew if I gave my family a reason to doubt that I could care for Sasha that they would surely do everything in their power to convince me to give her up to a more stable family. It took only a few days of intense training for her to understand that she wasn't allowed to "shit where she slept" (even though she still had accidents on occasion). However, controlling her behavior was nearly impossible, and nothing I ever did seemed to work. I tried everything I could think of and even the things I couldn't think of to curb her defiant nature. I listened to every suggestion including those that I despised, such as: an electric collar and isolation. Regrettably, I tried the electric collar but only days later tossed in the garbage and demanded my money back from the retailer and nearly knocked his teeth out in the process.

  The day my family arrived in Orlando; Florida was strange for sure. I remember I first saw my sister and brother-in-law who came to my new apartment during the afternoon. I recall that Sasha and I were waiting anxiously downstairs in the parking lot for them to arrive. Sasha was pulling hard against the leash and wanted me to let her go so she could tear up the flower garden in front of and adjacent building. Finally, to get her to calm down I picked herup and cradled her in my arms. After a few minutes I saw a car roll up and park in the nearest parking spot. A few seconds later my sister exited the driver's side of the car and a few moments after my brother-in-later exited from the passenger's side. I will never forget the look on my sisters face when she first saw Sasha. The only way I can describe it is - panic. I learned rather quickly that my sister did not like dogs. Though, she did call Sasha - "cute."

Later that night my parents came over and it was then that all Hell broke loose. From the moment my father sat down on the couch Sasha went bat shit bonkers trying to get his attention. She refused to listen to any command I gave her. She was so excited and jumped from the couch to floor then back to the couch and then back down onto the floor. I remember my father telling me, "You make her crazy, you know that, right?" He would thrust his arm out in front of him and say while holding back laughter, "I mean, you do look like a crazy person after all!" I would agree with him and reply while smiling, "Well, a dog does take after its owner after all."

That night my father took the only picture of me and Sasha when she a puppy. To this day I still have that image ingrained into my brain; I can describe every detail in that picture with my eyes closed. I remember it vividly. I was sitting at my computer desk (which was made of glass). I was holding Sasha around her belly while trying to balance her on my lap and keep her from turning her head. Her long floppy ears nearly covered her face. Her paws hung over my arm and her soft white belly was shining an exuberant white glow. It is that one picture; that image ingrained in my mind for all time that constantly reminds me what it was I am fighting to this very day. For And though I regret many of my actions while trying to house train her, discipline her and socialize her with her dogs, I can say with utmost certainly that she, like Gabbie is in fact my true soul mate. Make no mistake that they (Sasha and Gabbie) are undoubtedly my heart and soul...and always will be.

A DAY IN THE LIFE OF GABBIE: THE HAPPY DANCE

Over the years I have told many people that this day made all the others worth living. It began when I had returned to the vet to pick up Gabbie after an average check-up. I exited the car and gently closed the driver's door and pointed to Sasha who was climbing over the backseat and told her, "Relax, Sash. I'll be right back." My face illuminated with joy as I saw Gabbie sitting patiently on the curb outside the building. I threw my arms out to my sides and said with a streaking smile across my face, "Gabbers! What's up, baby girl?!" I was so happy to see Gabbie that I just couldn't contain my joy. I then looked to a woman who was holding Gabbie gently by her leash and nodded; it was the nurse. I looked back at my car as Sasha went into a frenzy; she wanted to greet Gabbie (and probably smell her rear end too). Sasha barked hysterically while racing from one side of the car to another hoping that she would find a way to unlock the door (the window was ajar slightly but she was too big to squeeze through). As I continued to walk forward and got closer and closer to Gabbie she seemed to become more and more excited. Suddenly, she leapt up onto to her rear legs like a bucking Bronco. Seconds later, she landed softly on her front paw. However, it was then that she did something she had never done before - The Happy Dance.

I walked up to the nurse and smiled warmly and immediately Gabbie thrust head between my legs; her way of hugging me (by now I was used to her getting me this way). The nurse seemed surprised even though it wasn't the first time she saw Gabbie do this to me. I leaned slightly forward and pet Gabbie on her side then hunched over and hugged her around her tightly around her belly. "Hey, Gabs! I missed you."

As I began to speak back and forth to the nurse and listen as she told me what I already knew; the results of her check-up, Gabbie began to bounce up and down; she was eager to get my attention. Off in the distance I heard saw winning loudly and periodically barking. I crouched down and balanced myself on the balls of my feet while looking at Gabbie who was widely jumping for joy. I smiled at her and said, "You wanna eat, girl? Is that it? You hungry?" Then without warning she paused momentarily barked loudly. I chuckled and seconds later she thrust forward and nearly knocked me over. I stood tall and said, "Okay, baby girl. We're going."

I took the leash from the nurse's hand and told her I would be back in a few moments to pay the balance; I wanted to put Gabbie in the car so Sasha would shut up. As I began to walk away, I heard the nurse say, "If only there were more people like you..." I stopped suddenly and turned around then replied, "If there were only more dogs like them." I glanced to the car and then looked down at Gabbie who was sitting patiently at my side. I continued, saying, "Then, it truly would be a perfect world." IA few seconds later I called to Gabbie and waved to the car and she took off like a bolt of lightning running eagerly to greet Sasha. I followed closely behind her and made sure there were no cars speeding by.

I opened the back door and Gabbie immediately jumped inside. Sasha wasted no time and began to smell her all over. Gabbie laid down and Sasha hovered over her and began to lick her ears without permission (but, Gabbie didn't seem to mind).

I told them I would return shortly and then gently closed the back door and walked back to the office. I entered the building and the nurse behind the counter looked up at me and then said, "She's an amazing dog!" She then handed me an invoice. I looked it over while saying, "You have no idea." After agreeing on the bill, I reached for my wallet and handed the nurse my debit card. She then swiped my card through the credit card machine and said, "She really loves you." I began to blush and replied, "I

would die for her," I paused and looked out through the glass of the front door and peered into the rear windshield of the car; Sasha was finally lying down. I then continued, "And, Sasha too. They're my daughters." The nurse handed me a slip to sign; I signed it without hesitation.

As I began to leave the building I asked, "Do I need to make another appointment?" The nurse replied, "Only if you want to?" I thought for a moment, "Let's do two weeks from today." The nurse nodded the said, "Sure. Do you need a reminder card?" I chuckled and replied, "Why not?" I took the reminder card and then turned and pushed the door slightly open. I held the door and said to the nurse, "By the way, thanks. Thanks for looking out for her..." The nurse smiled. She was about to speak when I continued and said, "If anything ever happened to her..." The nurse interrupted me, "You're welcome." I nodded and then turned back to face the door. I heard the nurse say, "Mr. Glick?" She asked. "Yea?" I replied. "You're a great dad." I was overwhelmed by her kind comments; my words got stuck in my throat. I pushed the door completely open while saying, "I'll see you in two weeks." I smiled then exited the building and walked back to the car.

I got in the car and adjusted the rear-view mirror. Sasha came up to me and climbed on top of the console. I gently grabbed her by one side of her jowls and pulled her close and kissed her on her nose. "I love you, Sash." She sat back down on the seat and panted heavily while smiling happily. Gabbie was laying in the back seat nearly asleep. "I love you, Gabs." I then started the car but before leaving I reached back behind me and pet Gabbie on her head. I looked at Sasha and then back to Gabbie. I was overcome with emotion as I told them, "It's us three forever, girls." I then turned back and re-adjusted the rear-view mirror and placed the gearshift in reverse. I tapped the gas petal and the slowly rolled back out of the parking spot.

As I began to drive on the main road, I lowered the rear windows completely and cranked the radio loud. Sasha thrust her head out one side and Gabbie rose slightly to sniff the air but quickly lost interest and laid back down and went to sleep.

"Heaven goes by favor. If it went by merit, you would stay out and your dog would go in."

- Mark Twain

CHAPTER FIVE
YOU LOOK LIKE A SASHA

People often ask me, "Drew, did you name your dogs?" I was always confused by this question. I often thought to myself, "They kinda named themselves actually." Sometimes people even insinuated that, "A guy always wants a masculine name for his dogs; a name that would intimidate people." To me that's a stupid thing to say. Why would I want people to be afraid of my dog? When I first debated on what to call, "Sasha" I thought about giving her a name that had meaning. Okay. Wait. Let me tell you a little more about Sasha's personality to help put things into perspective. Aside from the obvious she was extremely dominant (more than most dogs). She never turned away from a fight and she was even a sore loser. If she lost a wrestling match with me, she would stalk me for days waiting for me to drop my guard then pounce on me when I least expected it.

One day, well, actually it was more like a few days after I brought her home that I was looking at her with a smile on my face. I was watching her play and chase around an annoying squeaking ball across the living room floor. For some odd reason a random thought of Alexander, The Great popped into my head. I remembered my high school history teacher once told me that the female equivalent to Alexander, The Great is - Sasha. I told myself that, "She looks like a Sasha."

From that moment forward I called her, "Sasha", "Sash," and other abbreviations of the name. Though, I decided on that name for a much more legitimate reason. Due to her dominant nature and her relentless desire to conquer and win I felt the name was a perfect fit. I even told myself, "If I let her, she'll conquer the world." The name seemed almost natural as I spoke it. However, there was even a few moments when I tinkered with names like, Snow, Angel and, even, Baby. Ugh! To put it bluntly those names are awful. Just the thought of any of those names coming out of my mouth makes me want to slap myself silly. Can you imagine me yelling down the street, "Baby, get back here!" The odds are great that some random girl would have thought I was flirting with her and I surely would have ended up on the sidewalk in a fetal position moaning in pain.

Let me continue by telling you that on an average day I yelled at Sasha at least a hundred times. Sometimes I would yell, "Sasha! Get out of the damn garbage!" other times I yelled, "Sasha! Quit chewing on that chair leg!" There wasn't a day that went by that she didn't get into trouble. I used to tell her (Sasha), "You're the reason I can't have nice things." I was only joking, of course. Even though I wanted to pull my hair out of my skull her shenanigans made me laugh (but, it took a few days for me to do so).

I began to see that her destructive ways were something that I couldn't live without. I would tell my friends, "She keeps life interesting. I never know what I'm gonna walk into when I get home." I would laugh and smile every time I thought about coming home to find the garbage strewn across the floor (even though I would yell and scream). Sasha always looked so innocent (yea, right). She always tried to blame the mess on Gabbie. To this day I am confident that Sasha and Gabbie were in cahoots with one another. They made it impossible to punish them for the simple fact that I never knew who to punish. I even thought about putting a hidden camera in house just to get to the bottom of what was really going on.

There are more instances then I can recall when I stood with my arms out to my sides and asked, "What in the Hell did you two do?" Sasha would look at me as if to say, "I didn't do it!" Gabbie on the other hand would look confused and, even, disorientated. I often thought Gabbie was absent
minded; she always seemed to have this gleam in her eye where she was attempting to tell me, "Where am I? How did I get here?" However, I wasn't stupid, and I knew it was all an act.

Sasha was (and always will be) an incredibly intelligent dog. She knew how to "play the game." She watched everything I did, and I mean everything! She learned my strengths and my weaknesses. Eventually, she figured out that all she had to do to melt my heart was look at me with her big, bright eyes and I would hand her the world on a platter (I think she even taught Gabbie a trick or two) Over time, Sasha became synonymous with the word "destruction." Her devious ways seemed more humanlike then animal. People would often remark, "She gets that from you, Drew." I would laugh and on occasion even agree with them. However, no matter how rebellious she was, or rambunctious, or, even, destructive I never stopped loving her...and I never will.

"It is my life's mission to be as good of a person as my dogs already believe I am."

- Drew Glick

CHAPTER SIX
BONDED FROM BIRTH

Naming Gabbie was a bit more difficult then naming Sasha. Every time I thought I had found a suitable name it became obvious that it just wasn't a good fit after all. I remember a few nights after I brought Gabbie home I had asked my girlfriend to help me come up with a name once and for all. Sadly, she like I seemed to be tongue tied.

As the night went on the two of us were determined to stop calling her, "The Golden." I asked her over and over again, "What should she we call her?" But each time the only response I got was, "I don't know." Finally, I said, "What about Gabbie?" She thought about it for a moment then replied, "Why Gabbie?" To be honest I don't know why or "where" that named derived from? However, I was confident that I had finally found the perfect name. I smiled then pet Gabbie softly on the top of her head while saying, "She looks like a Gabbie." My girlfriend chuckled and replied, "If you say so."

It seemed to be fate that the name, "Gabbie" had come to me at all. I will never forget the first moment when Gabbie heard me call her, "Gabbie." She perked her ears and looked up at me as if she was waiting for me to continue speaking. I asked her while my girlfriend watched in amazement, "You like that name, girl?" Without hesitation, Gabbie smiled then barked once as if answering "yes." I was dumbfounded by her behavior. I wanted to ask her, "Can you understand me, girl?" I knew I had to keep such thoughts to myself; my girlfriend already thought I was crazy. I didn't want to encourage any more ridicules ideas from her any time soon. However, with each passing year it seemed that Gabbie and I were able to commune in ways that can only be described as, "spiritual."

Before continuing I want to say that over the years many people have commented to me about how "amazing" Gabbie is. And though it may seem out of context (and possibly spoiling any future books in this series) I want to tell a short story which occurred in December of 2015 while I was traveling cross country (with Gabbie) to the West Coast. It was early morning and it was bitter cold though the sun was shining bright. I was somewhere in the mid-west. I remember that I wanted to smoke as many cigarettes as possible before getting back into the car since I wasn't allowed to smoke. I was standing on a small patch of grass covered by a light coating of snow. Gabbie was beside me sniffing the grass and looking for a comfortable place to pee. I spied a young Asian man who was holding coffee and hurrying back to his room to escape the cold. He looked at me and then said hello, and then entered a room that was directly in front of me.

A few minutes later he exited the room and approached me and asked, "Is that your Dog?" I relied happily, "That's my Gabbie." I glanced over to Gabbie to see that was enjoying the cold weather and laying down on a patch of snow. The man then asked if he could pet her and I told him sure. He walked towards Gabbie then kneeled down and pet her on her head then looked back at me and asked, "Was she born with three legs?" I flicked my cigarette out into the street and casually walked closer to him and replied, "No, she had cancer when she was puppy." He seemed surprised, shocked almost.

He stood tall and took out his phone and then showed me a picture of his dog. "This is the weirdest thing," he said. I was confused and listened as he continued, saying, "Our dog just had his leg amputated; he has cancer too." I suddenly realized that meeting this man was no accident. He went on and asked me an array questions. He even told me that the doctor suggested that he not have the surgery performed and that he should allow his dog to pass on. I shook my head and told him that the same thing was said to me but that I refused to believe that Gabbie couldn't be saved. I told him I fought tooth and nail to get the doctor to listen to my pleas, and even admitted that on occasion I had to intimidate the doctor to do so. The man seemed relieved and told me how he worried endlessly about his dog, and that he even battled with thoughts that maybe he was putting his dog through more pain and suffering? I assured him that his dog would recuperate but told him that he needed to show no fear in front of his dog. I explained that he had to believe wholeheartedly that the surgery would be successful, or the dog would sense his worry and stop fighting.

After a minute or two he asked me if I could wait while he went to his room to get his wife? He was eager for her to meet Gabbie as well. I told him sure and then called to Gabbie and the two if us followed him to the door of his room. Gabbie sat down at my side and I pet her gently on her head and told her, "Good girl." We then waited for the man and his wife to return. A few seconds later the door opened, and the man introduced me to his wife, and I introduced her to Gabbie. She looked at Gabbie with amazement. She too seemed relieved to know that there was hope that her dog would beat the cancer.

The woman was overcome by emotions and said with tears forming in her eyes, "This is God's work." I asked her what she meant, and she replied, "We we're supposed to meet you and Gabbie. We asked for a sign and we got one." The woman then gave me a hug and told me that she appreciated the opportunity to meet Gabbie and I. A few seconds later, her husband extended his hand and I shook his hand with confidence. He waved to Gabbie and said goodbye to me while making his back into the room. He told me thank you and then the door closed and Gabbie and I headed to the car to escape the cold.

As I entered the car, I suddenly heard the man call to me from his room. I opened the car door and stepped out into the cold and pulled the collar of my coat over my face. He then shouted to me from across the grass, "Gabbie is an amazing dog!" I nodded and told him thank you and that I appreciated the kind words. "She inspires me," he said. I smirked and replied, "Me too." He then waved goodbye to me and shut the door to his room. I got back in the car and sat down in the seat; Gabbie was already half asleep. I leaned forward and pet her gently on her ribcage and told her, "I love you, Gab, Gab." I then leaned back and stared out the window; my mind was filled with thoughts of the future. However, I did periodically think back to what the man's wife had just said to me, "We asked for a sign and now we got one."

After all the experiences I had been through I started to become more and more confident that there were in fact unforeseen forces at work all around me; helping me and guiding me to where I was supposed to be. You see, meeting this man and his wife who had just been through the same pain as I endured over a decade earlier made me realize that even the most tragic things can become miracles, and like I said previously Gabbie and I had an uncanny ability to communicate without speaking. Most people as a matter of fact found this ability disturbing and would even ask, "How did you know that's what she wanted?" I would often laugh and reply, "I just know."

I have told many people about my strange ability to communicate with Gabbie on a subconscious level. Of course, they sneer at me and sometimes even scoff. Yet, I have always been able to prove my claim to having metaphysical powers by simply do exactly what I said I could. Though, many people still refused to believe their eyes. This fact is why they will continue to allow life to pass them and never truly enjoy the richness that life has to offer. For them money buy happiness when in reality is the exact opposite. As odd as it may sound, I even came cup with my own terminology to categorize this type of person. I labeled them as, "Impostors." Everyone else was given the title of, "Enlightened." Wait! I'm getting sidetracked, aren't I

As the years came and went, I was desperate to find a way to take New York; I wanted Gabbie to feel secure and happy. While doing so Gabbie and I briefly stayed with a friend of mine in Queens. A few weeks after arriving he watched me interact with Gabbie on a subconscious level and actually communicate with her and bridge the gap between human and dog. I remember that I was sitting on the floor and Gabbie had her head in my lap. I was brushing her coat and smoothing out the knots in her fur. Afterwards I laid next to her but propped myself up onto one elbow and then whispered in her ear. After a few seconds Gabbie turned her head backwards and looked into my eyes and I kissed her nose. She smiled and then laid down completely on the carpet and closed her eyes and began to fall asleep.

I gently let go of Gabbie and stood up while trying not to disturb her from her slumber. As I stood my friend asked me inquisitively, "What did you just do?" I looked over to him and with smirk on my face replied, "Talking to her, what else?" He smiled warmly at me and then stood up out of his chair and patted me on the back. He stood next to me for a few seconds the began to walk towards the kitchen. After a few steps he stopped suddenly and turned back to face me. He stood there for a few moments and said nothing; all he did was stare at me; I felt like he was trying to peer into my soul. He then said, "I never seen anyone love a dog like you do. It's absolutely amazing to watch you two."

I kneeled down and pet Gabbie on her ribcage and she inhaled a deep breath; that was here way of acknowledging that she understood. I then turned back to look at him and replied, "Well, I don't know what to say other then - she's not dog. She my daughter." His eyes began to water, and I listened as he replied, "That's why I love you, Drew. You're not like everyone else. You're different; better in a way even though you can be a real asshole sometimes." I chuckled and replied, "Well, no one's perfect." He roared with laughter.

After a few sentimental moments he then turned back to the kitchen and slowly walked forward while saying, "I'm glad you turned out to be the person I hoped you were." I was suddenly confused. I asked him what he meant, and he replied, "No matter how dark things get you never give up; you keep fighting." He pointed at Gabbie and continued, "Just like you've fought for Gabbie; it's inspiring." I quickly interjected and replied, "And Sasha. Don't forget I have two daughters." He smiled, "Of course! I could never forget about Sasha."

A few moments passed when suddenly random thoughts of Sasha ran wild in my mind. He immediately saw that I was becoming upset and apologized for upsetting me. I looked at him while trying desperately to hold back tears and said, "It's cool. "My only regret is that you never had a chance to meet her too. She would've loved you." He smiled at me and replied, "And I'm sure I would have adored her."

Suddenly he was overcome by emotion. I thought to myself that maybe I had said something to upset him? Did I perhaps remind him of something from his past? I didn't know. I then stood up and asked him, "Are you alright?" He turned to face the kitchen to hide his face; I was certain he was about to cry. I said nothing and just watched him as he made his way closer and closer to the kitchen. I figured our conversation was over, so I turned my attention back to Gabbie. I was just about to kneel down and give her a final kiss goodnight when I heard him call to me and say, "Don't hate yourself, Drew. People make mistakes. You're only human after all."

He stepped out of the kitchen with a plate of Macaroni and Cheese in one hand while bracing himself on the wall with the other. He shuffled carefully to the dining room table trying not to spill the Macaroni and Cheese on the floor then placed the plate down on the table and pulled the chair out from underneath and sat down. He sighed then turned and looked at me; his face had lost all expression. I was unsure of what he was looking at. He seemed suddenly upset but I couldn't be sure. Perhaps he was waiting for me to say something?

A few moments until he then turned slightly in the chair and showed me his palm and held his hand out in front of him and asked, "Can I have a cigarette, please?" I laughed and replied, "Why do you do that? I thought something was wrong. He asked again, "Please! Come on! Don't hold out on me!" I pointed at him and replied, "I thought you quit?" He scoffed at my remark and then sneered at me while saying, "I guess you're a bad influence on me after all, huh?" He lifted his arms and put his hands together in a praying position and pleaded with me to give him a cigarette.

I hesitated for a moment but then agreed and began to approach him from across the room. I took the pack of cigarettes from out of my front jean pocket and handed him a cigarette and told him, "Under one condition..." He interrupted me, "Ugh! What now?" He said jokingly. I glanced over to the kitchen, "You let me have some of that Mac and cheese?" In a swift motion he snatched the cigarette from my hand and replied while striking his lighter, "Have all you want." I hugged him and said thanks. As I walked into the kitchen, I saw him begin to blow smoke rings up to the ceiling (which he seemed to be ban expert at). "Damn, I love these things," he said while holding the cigarette up in front of him.

I licked my lips as I stood in the kitchen scooping up as much Macaroni and Cheese as I could until the plate was too heavy for me to carry. I then walked back over to the dining room table and sat down addict to him. As I was about to take my first bite into the warm, gooey Macaroni and Cheese my phone rang unexpectedly. The sound startled me, and I nearly dropped my fork to the floor. I patted my jean pockets and then eagerly took my phone out of my back pocket. I glanced down to the caller I.D. and instantly jumped up from my seat and told him, "I need to take this. I'll be right back." I then got up from the table and exited the apartment.

I got out into the hallway and answered the phone; my hand was quaking. I immediately said, "Thanks for calling me back." Then, a girl's voice, soft and low spoke to me through the phone and said, "Hi, Drew." I paced back and forth in the empty hallway. I was nervous but had no reason to be; I had spoken to her for over a month now. "How are you feeling today?" She asked. I held the phone to my ear then lowered my head and shut my eyes. "I wish I knew," I replied. I then felt a tear fall from one eye and roll down my cheek. My voice cracked as I continued, "I guess I'm feeling like shit." I sniffled then wiped my nose with the cuff of my sleeve and continued, "I miss her more every day."

After the conversation ended, I went back into the apartment. As I walked in, I saw my friend at the dining room table eating the macaroni and cheese which was now room temperature. I walked past him but stopped as I heard him call out to me and say, "Drew?" I turned and looked at him. He put the fork down on the edge of the plate and looked back over his shoulder and continued, "Are you okay?" He asked. I took a deep breath and then replied, "I will be." He then turned in his chair and held out his arms and said, "Will a hug help?" We looked at one another and somehow, we were speaking to one another even though our lips remained still. A few moments later I smiled warmly, and he smiled back.

PSALM OF COURAGE

Do not be frightened or worried:
for I am your God and I'm always beside you.

Be determined and confident:
since you are mine, I will always support you.

I am the God of love who moves on gently: leading
you on, drawing you into all that is new and lovely.

All you need is available now:
let me carry you and bear you along in safety.

I am the Lord of love who comes to you in quietness:
there's no need for struggle or panic, for I died for you
in the cruelty of torture: how can I let you suffer
alone?

I am the Spirit of love to direct you tenderly: I hold
your hand and I will not hurry you.

We will go on together into tomorrow:
for I am with you and I won't let you go.

Be not afraid for I am with you:
I shall never abandon you wherever you may fall.

Only be strong and very courageous:
for you are mine and I will always love you.

"The more I see of man, the more I like dogs."

- Mme. de Staël

CHAPTER SEVEN
FIND YOUR STRENGTH

Allow me to step away from the primary story if you will but only for a moment to say…

Many people will claim that there is no such thing as destiny; that every man, woman and child is granted the power of free will to do and say as they please. Thus, this ideology has birthed the common belief that we, humanity are the masters of our own demise. However, allow me to inject and explain to you what I have witnessed over the years. Destiny is real. Though, people often tend to stray from the path that God (the universe or whom or whatever you choose to call Him) has set forth for them to follow. This is simply due to their lack, or inability rather to stay headstrong and steadfast in the face of adversity. Their lack of faith becomes a cycle of unwanted self-destruction that all too often results with a mundane lifestyle and common existence.

If you follow the word of God, you will notice that on numerous occasions the words seem to be predicting something. Yet, like I have argued time and time again throughout this book you must prove your worthiness; you must show God that no matter the hardships you face will never allow you faith to fade.

Many people will read this book and become fearful, frightened even, that they themselves may one day find themselves in similar situations. They quake and clap their hands together in a praying position and look up into the sky and beg to never experience anything so traumatic during their lifetime. This in itself is a violation of God's teachings; the prophecy, if you will that He has predicted at the time of your birth.

Bruce Lee once said, "Do not pray for an easy life. Pray for the strength to overcome one." However, it seems that Bruce's' words were taken out of context. I believe that what Bruce was trying to say was not that you should endure one hardship after another with no glimmer of hope whatsoever. Yet, rather learn from the trials and tribulations that are faced with. In other words: do not become a statistic by remaining complacent, and, even, scared; fearing that you may jeopardize your livelihood if you refuse to challenge the forces that stand to deter you from success and happiness.

Today, we see a growing rise in the number homeless people who linger on the street corners of a large metropolis such as Los Angeles or New York.

Each and every day I walk down Sunset Boulevard and look at a man or woman with their hand out begging for spare change. They spend nearly twelve hours a day pleading for salvation only to be shunned and ignored by their fellow man.

Many people have told me, "Drew, you are different; you are in tune with the universe, or whatever you want to call it." The difference between me and the people who say such things [to me] is that I know with the utmost certainty that nothing is a coincidence. Everyone else on the other hand sees everything as random; unimportant - unless they can post it on their Facebook page, that is. To truly understand, or better yet predict the outcome of your choices you must learn to "connect the dots." You must expand your mind to the possibility that you are right where you are supposed to be - even if you find yourself facing grueling challenges and soul crushing anguish.

To truly achieve a state of enlightenment you have to be conscious of your surroundings. You must see things differently and lift the veil that conceals your vision from the truth - your ultimate destiny. Only you know who and what you are supposed to become. I'm sure you can feel it. That somehow it calls out to you. You can deny it all you want but no matter how much you try to run and hide it will find you; it [destiny] will stalk you until you decide to face it. Only then will you prove your worthiness and enter the gates of the "Golden Palace..."

…In time, you will understand what I mean...

"A dog is not "almost human" and I know of no greater insult to the canine race than to describe it as such."

- John Holmes

CHAPTER EIGHT
STRENGTH BEYOND STRENGTH

PT. 1:
GAME OF DEATH

Would you like to play a game? What is your wager? How about your soul?...

Sadly, the remaining chapters of this book will not be easy for many readers to read. In fact, I wouldn't blame you if you put this book down and refused to pick it up again for months, years, or never at all. I have already told you about the day that I brought Sasha home for the pet store. Though, I haven't told you about the day Gabbie came home
    (I've only briefly mentioned short moments after I had already adopted her). Nor have I told you about

the aftermath of her surgery, how "we" survived it, and inevitably how we, well, no, rather how, Gabbie beat the odds. I guess this is as good of a time as any to start to do so...

Let me take you back now to the beginning; to the very beginning, that is. This may be hard for many readers to believe but in the early days when I first introduced Gabbie to Sasha, Gabbie hated me but seemed to adore Sasha. In fact, she (Gabbie) often growled at me and even ran from me when I tried to approach her; she even bit me a few times (but I bit her back). Though, as I would soon learn it wasn't me that she hated. In fact, as you will read it was human beings overall that she distrusted. Of course, she never told me this - Cesar Millan did. No, I'm only kidding. Believe it or not a local trainer told me after weeks of intense obedience training.

At twenty-four weeks old she (Gabbie) had already struggled beyond belief. A few weeks before I adopted her, she was adopted by another family. However, for whatever reason they returned her forty-eight hours later as if she was a broken iPod (I'll keep my thoughts about that family to myself). Though, somehow, I knew without knowing that Gabbie's journey from one home to another was indeed a turn for the better; it was a blessing in disguise.

I recall sitting on my living room floor and watching Sasha as she pounced repeatedly on top of Gabbie trying to bully her (she was only playing, of course). Honestly, Gabbie had no desire to play. It seemed strange to me that Gabbie would just "sit there and take it." Finally, Sasha gave up and went to her bed and laid down.

The first few nights Gabbie was home she wasn't much more than just a statue made of "gold." As the first forty-eight hours came and went, I began to worry that she wouldn't be able to adapt to her new surroundings. She didn't do much of anything other than seem to be watching me, staring at walls and looking out windows. When it came time to take her outside, she refused to go, and often times peed on the carpet (but each time she did she tried to hide it by urinating in the corner).

A day or so later I called the vet and asked them if I was doing something wrong? The vet replied, "No. Sometimes it just takes time." However, I had an awkward feeling that there was an underlying problem that I hadn't discovered yet. For the next week Gabbie peed all over the house; it infuriated me. I began to feel like she was doing it on purpose. I lashed out at her and yelled while grabbing her by her lush mane and told her, "Outside! Pee outside!" I often regret being overly aggressive with both her and Sasha when they were puppies. But I was young and stupid, and I didn't know any better.

At twenty-six years old I had no idea what I was doing when it came to house training two dogs. Often times I felt overwhelmed and overburdened. However, I was aware enough (unlike other people) to know that I had willingly taken on this responsibility, and that I had to follow through on the commitment no matter how hard things became (and things were about to get harder than I could ever imagine).

Over the next few weeks Gabbie seemed to become more defiant. I was becoming frustrated and my girlfriend repeatedly said, "Maybe she just doesn't like us?" I often told her that something seemed to be wrong. It was almost as if Gabbie was being defensive; like she was protecting herself from a predator. Upon further investigation many dogs' owners told me, "A dog will hide its pain." I began to think that maybe that was true for Gabbie? There were no obvious signs of trauma. So, I began to consider that I would have to take her to the vet for a checkup. The only problem was I did not have the financial means to do so. I told myself, "If I have to burn the bill so be it."

I called the vet a few days later and asked them if I could schedule an appointment for Gabbie. They asked me, "What's going on with her?" I didn't even know how to respond to the question for the simple fact that I had no idea if there was anything wrong with her in the first place. I explained that she was peeing all over the house and appeared to be in a state of distress. The vet told me, "It's natural for a dog feel like an outcast when they enter a new home. Give it's few more weeks and if things don't change call us back." I said, "Okay" then hung up the phone. However, after a few seconds I picked the phone back up and again called the vet.

As the receptionist answered the phone, I interrupted her and said, "Listen. This is Mr. Glick again. Gabbie needs to be seen today. I'll be there in fifteen minutes" I began to hang-up the phone but raised it back up to my ear and said, "...and please don't dismiss me like that again." The girl on the other end of the phone started to speak but I hung up quickly and then immediately called for Gabbie. Her behavior, this time changed drastically (this was the first time she came to me on her own free will when I called her). "Come on, Gabs," I called out across the kitchen. "We're going to the doctor." I then turned around to find Gabbie next to me waiting patiently. I bent forward and pet her on her belly, and then attached the leash to her collar (it is a pink collar that she has to this day).

I opened the door and the sun burst in; it was hot but then again, I was in Florida. Gabbie pushed her way passed me; she was eager to go even though she didn't know where we were going. She rushed down the stairs and yanked the leash from my hands. I called to her, but she continued to scurry down the stairs; she was graceful even when slipped and nearly fell. Strangely, when she got the bottom of the stairs she turned and faced me (I could swear she was smiling). She then looked up at me and waited patiently at the bottom of the stairs. I smiled at her and said out loud, "Okay, Gabs. I'm coming."

I walked Gabbie to the car (which was parked directly out front of my apartment). It was rare that I got so lucky. More often than not I had to park acrossthe lot or around the corner. Gabbie pulled me harder and harder as we got closer to the car. I took my keys out of pocket and Gabbie barked. I looked down at her with a surprised look on my face, "I thought you hated the car, Gabs? I asked aloud. She looked up at me and her ears turned backwards as if she was listening to something behind her.

I opened the back-passenger's door and Gabbie leaped into the back seat. I was a bit shocked because she never was so eager to go for a car ride. As a matter of fact, she often vomited and seemed agitated each time she rode in the car regardless of how far were going. After she was settled in, I gently closed the door and walked to the driver's door. As I opened the door, I felt a cool breeze brush up against me; it was an odd feeling and I was overcome by a dreadful sensation.

I sat in the driver's seat and adjusted the rear-view mirror, "How you doing, Gabs?" I asked her. She turned and looked back at me in the mirror. She seemed to be saying, "Let's just go already!" I put the key in the ignition and started the car. The vet wasn't far away but still I felt a need to hurry. We drove for under ten minutes until I pulled into the driveway at the clinic. Gabbie got excited and put her head out the window (I had the window halfway down hoping the cool air would keep her from getting car sick). I quickly put the car in park and opened the back door and let Gabbie out. Before I could put the leash on, she leapt out and ran to the front door. of the building. I yelled to her, "Gabbie! Where you going?" (I was glad there were no cars coming though still I felt that I was irresponsible and should secured the leash before I opened the door).

She got to the front door before me and I could see people inside looking out into the parking lot; I'm sure they were wondering why a stray dog was watching them through the glass? I approached Gabbie and pet her on her back the opened the door. I tried to restrain her, but she squeezed her snout into the door frame and forced the door open. She ran inside and jumped on top of the counter. The receptionist chuckled and said, "You must be Gabbie?" However, Gabbie wasn't interested in making her friends. Rather she wanted the treats that were on the countertop. In a swift motion she used her snout and pushed a tin canister to the edge of the countertop; it came crashing down onto the floor moments later. I threw one hand up to my forehead and said, "I'll pay for that." The receptionist laughed and replied, "Don't worry. It happens all the time."

I gently grabbed Gabbie by the collar and told her to "heel" and then held her securely at my side. I told the receptionist, "I'm Mr. Glick. I called you earlier." The receptionist typed on her compeer then replied while staring into the screen, "Yes. I remember you." She turned to look at me. I felt embarrassed. I tried to justify my behavior by saying, "I'm sorry if I offended you earlier it's just..." She interrupted me and said, "I understand. She's your baby."

Gabbie turned to group of people who were waiting quietly in the waiting area (there were a few dogs as well) and began to wag her tail back and forth. She barked wildly (only for a minute) and a few of the dogs barked back. I asked Gabbie (though I knew she couldn't understand me), "Gabs? Why are you so excited?" The young girl behind the counter handed me a clipboard and asked me to fill out a few medical papers, and then politely asked me to sit and wait for the doctor.

I tugged on the leash and Gabbie followed me to the nearest seat. She sat patiently but I could tell she was waiting for me to lower my defenses (I knew that the moment I let go of the leash she would run off; probably to where the other dogs were?). It was hard for me to write because Gabbie was tugging on the leash. A few minutes later I saw a girl dressed in all blue walk through a door which lead into the examination area. She called out, "Gabbie?" I raised my hand and replied, "Here." I felt like I was in high school responding to roll call. I stood up and said, "Come, Gabs." Gabbie smiled and looked up at me then followed me into through the door and into the back.

We entered a small ten by ten room and the girl in blue (which I assumed was a nurse of some kind) asked me an array of questions. First, she asked, "Is she spayed?" I replied, "Yes." Then she asked, "Does she have her shots?" I replied in a curious tone, "What shots do you mean?" She listed off various types, saying, "What I mean is - rabies, distemper...." I told her, "Oh, yea. She has all that." She turned and wrote on a white piece of paper attached to a clipboard, "Is she on any heart worm medicine?" She asked me while focusing on the clipboard and taking notes. I replied, "Yea, she takes it once a month." I was struggling to hold Gabbie still. The nurse then took the clipboard off the counter and placed it under her arm then said,

"Okay. The doctor will be in shortly." I smiled at her and replied, "Great! We'll be here."

I walked Gabbie to a chair that was pressed tightly into the corner of the room. I sat down and Gabbie sat down in front of me. The silence in the room was overwhelming. I thought to myself, "They really need some kind of music in here." After a few minutes of waiting the door opened and the doctor came in. Gabbie wagged her tail and pulled against the leash; she was excited. The doctor pet her and kneeled down and began to look inside her mouth and in her ears. "She a happy pup...You're doing a good job with her," the doctor said while looking at me. I nodded then replied, "I've only had her for a few weeks...but, thanks."

The doctor stood up and motioned to the nurse. The nurse looked at me and asked if I could help get Gabbie on the scale. I told her it would be my pleasure and then coaxed Gabbie onto the scale. I heard the nurse call out, "81 pounds." I thought to myself, "81 pounds? That can't be right?" The doctor then turned to me, "What kind of food does she eat?" I thought for a second then replied. "Pedigree, I believe." The doctor pet Gabbie on the top of her head while asking, "And she is eating okay?" I suddenly had a sinking feeling in the pit of my stomach. "Yea, no worries there. She loves to eat as a matter of fact." The doctor nodded then asked me to explain what was going on; the problems that I was incurring while trying to house train Gabbie.

I told the doctor that she refused to go outside to pee and how her behavior seemed "defensive." I explained that she seemed moody throughout the day and, even, grumpy. The doctor replied by telling me what I already knew. Again, I heard the fateful words, "She just may need time to adjust." I lowered my head; I was becoming frustrated. I then gritted my teeth and tried desperately to hold back my emotions (which were ready to erupt at any moment). I told the doctor, "Listen, you're a doctor..." I looked at Gabbie though had no idea why I did; I felt like she was calling to me. I then looked back up at the doctor and continued, "Why is it you can't see something's wrong?" The doctor seemed insulted by my remark, "Mr. Glick, " he said in a strong tone, "Most dogs rebel in the beginning; they want to be the alpha."

I couldn't believe how ignorant this doctor was. I replied back and this time began to make demands, "I'm telling you something's off..." He tried to speak but I refused to allow him a moment to interject. "Listen," my voice grew loud, "I'm trying to tell you something's wrong. Do I really need to contact the ASPCA and tell them how you refuse to treat my dog?" The doctor seemed shocked that I would resort to threats. "Mr. Glick, please try and understand..." I lashed out and shouted back, "Stop it!" The nurse became frightful and the doctor just stood there (I couldn't tell if he was frozen by fear or just plain coldhearted). I continued, "I'm sorry..." I apologized even though I felt like I shouldn't have. "I'm worried, that's all. I know something is wrong." He interrupted me and asked,

"How do you know?" I felt like he was patronizing me. I pursued my lips and said strongly, "I just know."

The doctor exhaled a heavy breath and I got the impression he thought I was stupid. He then placed his hands in his pockets and told me, "Mr. Glick I hate to say this, but you are too bonded to Gabbie." I couldn't believe what I just heard. I asked him with anger in my voice, "Are you serious?" He stared at me refusing to be intimidated (though, I wasn't trying to intimidate him). "Listen," he said. "If you want, I can run some tests. But I really think you should give it some time. Let her adjust, I mean." I then gripped the leash tight, "Yes, run tests. I know I'm right."

The doctor told me to wait for him to return and asked me to be patient. I sat with Gabbie in the examination room for what seemed like an eternity. Then, the door then opened and the doctor entered. I saw him carrying a syringe; the nurse followed behind him with a tray filled with all sorts of medical instruments. I put my arm in front of Gabbie to shield her and asked, "What is all that?" The doctor replied with a condescending tone, "You want me to run some tests, right?" I nodded my head and stuttered my words, "Yea, but..." The nurse placed the tray onto the counter and the doctor replied, "I need to draw some blood..." I interrupted him, "Blood?!" I exclaimed. "For what?" The doctor picked up the syringe while saying, "Its standard procedure, Mr. Glick." He stepped forward to Gabbie then looked at me and continued, "Please try and relax."

I dropped my arm then told Gabbie, "It's okay, Gabbers. I won't let anyone hurt you." The doctor kneeled down and the nurse came over and held Gabbie still. I told the nurse, "Maybe it's better if I hold her? She knows me and..." The nurse looked to me and said while trying to focus on keeping Gabbie still, "Don't worry. I do this all the time." I sat back in the chair and muttered, "Sure you do." A few moments passed and the doctor called out, "All done." The nurse let go of Gabbie and the doctor stood up. Gabbie turned to me and jumped into my lap; she was happy. She licked my face and I laughed then placed her gently down onto the floor. The nurse was watching us; she had a smile streaking across her face, but it was obvious she was trying to hide it.

The nurse gathered up the tray and then said, "She really seems to love you." I stood up and pet Gabbie then replied, "She's my baby..." Suddenly, Gabbie pushed me with her snout. I laughed and called out, "Gabs! What are you doing?" Gabbie then thrust her head between my legs; I was
embarrassed. I thought maybe she smelled the remnants of the day old treat I had in my pocket. The nurse began to laugh. "Gabs! Gabs! Please, boo bear, you're gonna knock me over..." I said while trying to block Gabbie. The nurse walked to the door then turned to me and said, "She trying to hug you." I was confused, "Hug me?" I told Gabbie to sit then continued, "Are you serious?" I asked the nurse curiously.

A few moments later a voice called to the nurse from the busy hallway; it was the doctor telling the nurse to hurry. "Like I said, Gabbie loves you," the nurse told me while I looked down to Gabbie and pet her. I said nothing just stood there deep in thought. "Good luck, Mr. Glick." The nurse's voice echoed around me as if time itself was slowing down. "You really are doing a great job with her." I hesitated but for only a moment then smiled and said thank you and the nurse left the room.

PSALM OF HOPE

Help me, God, to look ahead more hopefully:
nothing like a death sentence to concentrate my
mind.

I'm told I ought to plan for years ahead:
but to settle for the next six months could be more
creative.

If I could fix my sights on the immediate future:
then I might get priorities in order.

The future can be deadly and uninviting: it's easy to
postpone the important thing for a rainy day.

But this life's not a rehearsal:
it's the only performance I've got; help me now to be
what I'd like some day to become, for faiths about
this life not another one: religion not only for
the next world, but for this!

Come, Holy Spirit, fill this moment: grant me, God, to
be really myself, to know today is always my meeting
with you: to live this day as if it were my last.

"If a dog will not come to you after having looked you in the face, you should go home and examine your conscience."

\- Woodrow Wilson

CHAPTER NINE
STRENGTH BEYOND STRENGTH

PT. 2
HEADFIRST INTO HELL.

Winston Churchill once said, "If you are going through Hell, keep going." I can't tell you why I refused to give up; to do what most people would surely call the "humane thing." But, would it have been humane? To give up, I mean. All I knew was that something told me that I was supposed to keep going. I knew without knowing that Gabbie was meant to live; that she would beat the cancer and become a "miracle" (as she has often times been called). The day I stood in the examination room where the doctor told me every possible worst case scenario on why surgery was a bad choice the more I knew surgery was the only choice. I told myself I would do anything and everything to make sure Gabbie survived even if it meant I had to go to Hell so she could do so. As I would soon come to find out this so called "Hell" was nightmarish in every sense of the word. Yet, as unrelenting as it was, as painful as it was; heartbreaking and soul wrenching alike I remained steadfast, and by the time I found my way out of this Hell that I so willingly chose to endure my life took a whole new meaning.

The more I dwelled on it the more I came to realize that what I found in that place, Hell to be exact was something unexpected; something I never looked for or thought was possible to find. This "something" however, cannot be bought no matter how much money you have, and it cannot be bartered with regardless of how much gold you offer to trade. It is not acquired through business transactions, college degrees or intelligence but rather through faith.

Almost immediately those people who doubted Gabbie's strength; who mocked me and my resolve; the weak and soulless human beings that told us it couldn't be done would realize that anything is possible. Though, this awakening (as I often times refer to it) would not come from my deeds, my sacrifice, endless love, or even, from my undying support for Gabbie. Yet, rather it would come from Gabbie herself.

I often heard people comment as if they were jealous, "Drew, there's something different about you." I guess these people (perhaps those people who read my past novels) were more stubborn then I first assumed? In my past books I have written about the unseen forces that surround us every day. More often than not I preach, "The only way to find God is to first find yourself." Though, no matter how convincing I may be my words fall on deaf ears. Why? Isn't it obvious? Simply put no one wants to sacrifice. Almost everyone you meet will say how they want something so badly and would do anything to get it. Still, none of these people want to sacrifice to get the "something" they so desperately desire.

It may seem like I am going off topic but bear with me for a moment longer. Let me tell you a simple truth that many people are too ignorant to accept. I have come to learn that throughout the course of our lives we all will quest for many things. Then one day we, or rather a person will quest for "something" that has no name. Many people fail to realize that when you begin your quest for this "something" you must do so because it is your heart's desire. In other words, the "something" you search for must fill a hole in your heart, even complete your soul in a sense.

Before I had my so-called epiphany, I was like most other people who tried to make sense of the divine though more often than not seemed incapable of doing so. As I look back on it now, I never knew that I was on quest to find the missing pieces of my heart. To this day I don't know how it even began or why. However, over the years I have come to realize one fact that is both disturbing and sad: this "something" is what most people relentlessly search for, and something which even more people will never find. The difference between me and the rest of the rest of the world's population is that my "something" found me. Then again maybe that's not as uncommon as I think it is. Perhaps I just had the foresight to see the "something" that consumed my life like a hurricane, and the willingness to sacrifice for the "something" I wanted?

I'm sure that in due time you, the reader will agree with me when I say that whatever it was that God wanted me to discover in that pit of darkness eventually became a vision of the future. In time the Hell that I had experienced became a blessing. Unbeknownst to me, however, Gabbie would become far more than just a dog. Before I knew it, she would be an inspiration to dog lovers everywhere...and, even, to other dogs...

It was sometime during the summer (exactly when I can't remember). For weeks I had butterflies in my stomach. Each day I found myself confronted by life altering choices; not for me but for Gabbie. I stayed awake night after night desperate to find an answer; praying for a sign to know if what I was doing was the right thing. I feared that I may be exposing Gabbie to further pain and suffering? My thoughts ran wild and I continued to battle with the possibility of euthanasia.

A few days earlier my heart sank into my stomach when I was told, "Gabbie has cancer." As I heard those words come through the phone I froze. I thought back to a few months earlier, to the time Gabbie and I were in the clinic; to the day I stood over Gabbie like a Tiger protecting its young and demanding that the doctor help her. Now she was stricken with cancer, Osteosarcoma to be exact. There was no magic cure that could would make it go away. This time I worried she wouldn't be able to overcome it. The odds of beating it were one in a trillion.

Following the devastating news (which the doctor gave me with ease) I immediately drove to the hospital leaving skid marks on the concrete as I sped through the neighborhood. I remember the feeling that overcame me as I drove for a few miles which felt like a cross country trek. During those few brief moments I had suddenly found myself unwillingly thrust in a place I can only describe as Oblivion; a metaphorical prison that was now encasing me completely. It seemed like I was daydreaming; I saw a figure that resembled the Grim Reaper standing before me. I suddenly felt like death was stalking me; taunting me to fight a battle I couldn't win. However, I was determined to try.

This endless battle began when I entered the hospital (the animal hospital, of course) and the receptionist at the counter (a different receptionist this time) told me to be patient and please sit and wait to be called. I nodded and sat in the nearest seat to the doorway leading into the examination room. A few minutes later the doctor came out (this time a male doctor) and called for me, "Mr. Glick?" He asked. Just like last time I raised my hand and got up out of my chair. "Follow me, please." He said while he pushed opened the swinging door. I sped up my walk (trying not to be obvious) and rushed into the back and shut the door behind me.

I entered the small ten by ten room and waited for the doctor to speak. He seemed hesitate and I got the feeling he was waiting for me to speak first. He placed his hands in his coat pockets and said with a heavy breath, "Mr. Glick I'm sorry but..." I turned to face the wall and cupped one hand over my mouth. I heard him ask, "Mr. Glick? Are you okay?" I turned back around and looked at him while gritting my teeth, "Am I okay? Of course, I'm not okay!" I felt possessed; my voice was not my own; I felt like the devil had suddenly erupted from within me.

He took his hands out of his pockets and then flipped a switch on the side of an aluminum box (attached to the wall by a device which gripped it tightly on all sides). Instantly, a light came on; I saw Gabbie's x-ray. The doctor cleared his throat then said, "We can't tell if the cancer has spread yet." He paused waiting for my reaction, but I had none. He then continued, "At this point I don't think surgery is a good option." I walked forward and looked at the x-ray closely then turned and snarled at him and replied, "Are you telling me to give up on her?" He carefully backed away from me. The look in my eye must have frightened him. He then spoke to me with conviction in his voice, "It's a fact that ninety percent of dogs with this type of cancer never survive..."

Without warning I smashed my fist on the aluminum table next to me; the sound reverberated off the walls startling the people waiting in the foyer, "Gabbie won't die!" I shouted back at him. His eyes widened. He was surprised by my sudden outburst. I saw him swallow hard; he was nervous but, he refused to show it. I pointed at him and cut through the air with one hand like a knife through butter. I continued, saying, "If I have to go to Hell to save her then show me where I can buy a ticket."

He carefully walked back to the x-ray and replied, "Mr. Glick," he then turned off the light, "I know how you feel..." I interjected and yelled, startling him again, "Do you!? Do you know how I feel!?" He said nothing only stared at me with a blank expression on his face, "Try and understand," he then put his hands back into his coat pockets, "This cancer cannot be beat. If it's already spread, then..." My voice cracked; I tried to speak but the words were stuck in my throat. I repeatedly cleared my throat and tried desperately to hold back tears. I blurted out, "Take her leg if you have to...," a tear fell uncontrollably down my cheek; I couldn't hold back my emotions any longer. "But she will not die!" I insisted. The doctor exhaled a heavy breath and then reached for the x-ray and took it down then placed it back into a manilla envelope. He couldn't even look at me as he said, "If that's what you want."

As he began to walk to the door he looked back over this shoulder and said, "Even if I take her leg there are no guarantees." I reached into my jacket pocket and took a cigarette from the pack and placed it behind my ear, "I'm not asking you for a guarantee..." I stared intently into his eyes hoping to see a glimpse of empathy; I saw only a black void of emptiness. I looked him up and down while telling him, "Just do what you have to, and I'll do the rest." The doctor left the room and I waited a few minutes before leaving to go home. Even though he didn't know it, yet I was going to get Gabbie and then bring her back to the clinic later that afternoon to have the surgery performed.

About twenty minutes later I had arrived home and rushed to get Gabbie ready. I packed her toys and even a t-shirt with my scent on it so she would know I was with her. I carefully picked up Gabbie held her in my arms; my backpack was hanging off one shoulder. A voice called to me from behind; it was my girlfriend. "Where are you going?" She asked. I turned around and said while holding Gabbie, "To the vet. Their gonna amputate her leg today." Her face went white as if she had just seen a ghost. "What?!" She exclaimed. "Were you not going to tell me?" She asked angrily. I shook my head side to side and replied, "How fucking stupid are you? I told you! You ignored me, remember?" She said nothing and just remind quiet.

I walked to the couch only a few feet away and gently placed Gabbie down on the soft cushion and then kissed her on her nose. I adjusted my backpack while turning back to look at my girlfriend. "Listen to me," I told her. "I don't care if you want to ignore me, even abandon me but I won't let you do it to Gabs." She was awe struck. She scowled at me and asked, "How did I abandon you?" It was obvious that she hadn't been listening to me all times that I told her that her support was all I needed to help me deal with my emotions.

I looked at Gabbie then back to her. "That's exactly what I mean." She quickly interjected, "What?"

I turned the doorknob and let the sunshine in; I was trying to leave but she was forcing me to stay. I gritted my teeth while telling her, "This isn't about me. Not anymore." I sighed heavily. "Don't you get it?" I asked her rhetorically. She crunched her eyes; I guess she was confused? She replied, "But, you just said..." I stepped forward and she immediately stopped talking. She swallowed hard; the look in my eyes could have burn through steel. I then continued, "What I said was that Gabbie needs you. It's obvious to me now that you don't care." I then walked to the couch and put my hands under Gabbie's belly; I was going to pick her up and bring her to the car because I didn't want her walking in her condition.

As I lifted Gabbie off the couch I heard my girlfriend say to me from behind, "You're taking what I said the wrong way." I held Gabbie in my arms and turned back to look at her. "Maybe I am." I replied. She placed her hands on her hips and rolled her eyes. "But, if you believe that you are right and I am wrong," I then took a step to the door making it obvious I had no intention on staying and then asked her facetiously, "Then why are we still having this conversation?" She looked at me and said as a child would who was playing coy to keep from being punished, "What do you mean?" She asked me with a tone of resentment in her voice. I scoffed and then asked her angrily, "Don't you see what's going on?"

She stood in front of me like a deer caught in headlights saying and said nothing. I thought momentarily that perhaps she was even concocting some kind of excuse. I made my way to door and pushed open the screen with my shoulder. I lowered my head and shut my eyes. A few seconds later my eyes sprung open and I was suddenly filled with immense rage. "Gabbie is dying!" I shouted as I turned back and stared into her eyes. I then continued and said, "I won't let that happen!" Then, in a swift motion I shoved the door open with my shoulder. While walking to my car I said aloud, "If it costs me everything I own, everything I am she will not die." I grunted then told her in a stern voice, "Not like this, you hear me?" I then placed Gabbie gently down on the lawn and gave her a moment to rest; my arms were getting sore.

I hadn't yet realized that my girlfriend had followed me halfway down the driveway muttering all sorts of incoherent words which were too indistinct for me to hear. She continued to speak but I wasn't focused on what she was saying, nor did I care. I then opened the back-driver's side door then picked up Gabbie and carefully placed her onto the seat. I shut the door trying not to slam it and opened the driver's door wide. Before I got in, however, I turned to face my girlfriend and asked her, "Will you ever learn to care about someone other than yourself?" Again, she snarled at me and without a word retreated back up the driveway. As I got into the driver's seat, she began to talk to me, but I quickly started the ignition and revved the engine to drown out her voice; I didn't want to hear her excuses anymore.

She watched me back out of the driveway and I continued to glance into the rear-view mirror until she was completely out of sight. I adjusted the mirror and looked at Gabbie. I smiled to her and she seemed to smile back. "It's okay, baby girl," I told her. "I won't let anything happen to you." A few moments later, Gabbie began to pant heavily. I suddenly recalled the vet telling me, "Watch her for labored breathing." I began to panic. "She's getting worse," I thought. I continued to look at Gabbie through the rear-view mirror trying to speak to her telepathically. I wasn't aware that I was approaching a red light. however. I turned my attention back to the road and pressed the brake pedal harder than normal and the car came to an abrupt stop. I looked ahead of me and noticed there didn't seem to be many cars on the road at that time. I found it odd since it was the middle of the day. I took a deep breath and I muttered, "Lord, I'm begging you." I rolled my palms over the top of the steering wheel; I was nervous and sweating profusely. "My baby girl needs you." Tears formed behind my eye and moments later I felt them roll down my cheeks, "Please help her," I pleaded. My voice was low and monotone as I continued to mutter prayers (which ones I can't recall).

I continued to drive all the while glancing in the rear-view mirror. I could feel Gabbie staring at me. Her eyes were fixated on me in the mirror. Strangely, she seemed happy and excited. I thought that maybe I was overreacting; maybe she wasn't sick? I couldn't shake the feeling that something was wrong. After a few minutes I looked at Gabbie in the rear-view mirror and asked her, "You trying to tell me something, Gabs?" It was odd but I could hear her in my head. It was as if she was reading my thoughts. After a minute or two she got up and placed her chin down on the console; she seemed suddenly saddened.

I reached behind the seat and petted her gently. Within seconds she jolted upright and her demeanor changed almost instantly. She barked once; which startled me and made me jerk the wheel slightly in one direction. "Gabs!" I exclaimed. "What's the matter?" I asked her. Then, in a swift motion she went to the window and fell up against the back seat and stared out the window. "You want me to put the window down? Is that, girl?" I pressed the power button and lowered the rear passenger windows. She inched forward but don't stick her entire head out the window, only her snout. She sniffed the air and then as if she didn't like what she smelled laid back down on the seat and shut her eyes.

I saw the animal clinic off in the distance and pressed the gas pedal harder; I was anxious to arrive. "Here we go." I muttered. I turned the steering wheel and entered the driveway of the animal clinic and pulled into the nearest parking spot Once stopped I put the gearshift on park and took the key from the ignition. Gabbie got excited and stood up and again placed her snout out the window of the car. I turned slightly and threw my arm over the headrest of the passenger's seat then twisted my neck and turned and looked back at her. I called her name and she snapped her head and looked at me with a glare in her eye. I listened as she panted then told her, "I'll be right here, Gabs. I won't leave you."

She then casually turned back to the window and continued to sniff the outside air. I looked at her intently and said reassuringly, "I love you, Gabs." She then barked out the window as she saw another dog walking with its owner at the other end of the parking lot. I chuckled then took off my seatbelt and said, "Okay, we're going."

PSALM OF PRAYING

I don't know how to pray:
my God, you're far away from me.

The words don't come easily anymore:
phrases I know by heart don't seem
so genuine.

My energy is drained, you don't feel near me:
dryness and boredom have taken a hold on me; I
know you're close, but I cannot see you:
*you seem to be here, but out *
of focus.

My life's full of tensions, I'm not able to relax:
stresses and strains make me certain I
cannot cope.

God, you are nearer to me than my breathing: yet my
heart goes blank and my mind won't grasp you.

Others have travelled this road before:
why do I have to struggle to find the way for myself?

Be close to me again, let me feel your presence:
help me hold my mind in my heart, give life to the dry
bones of my will: bring renewal to my tired
understanding, then I'll thank you with
all my power: and praise you from
the depths of my being.

"Man is a dog's idea of what God should be."

- Holbrook Jackson

CHAPTER TEN
STRENGTH BEYOND STRENGTH

PT. 3
THE DARKEST PART OF HELL IS THE BRIGHTEST

It was a few days following Gabbie's surgery (at the time I was living in Harmony, Florida) when I found myself sitting on my couch and listening as my girlfriend said, "Gabbie's fine now." Her tone was callous and insensitive, and I refused to look at her. I'm not sure if we had an argument earlier but her remark was nothing less than ignorant. I stayed sitting on the couch while she was stood across the room and looked directly at me; he eyes burning into the back of my skull. I said nothing to her; I just sat there staring into the lights in the ceiling. I turned my attention to Gabbie and smiled and moments later Gabbie smiled back. Seeing Gabbie in that state with staples protruding off one side of her body changed me. It made me see just how vulnerable she was; how vulnerable we all are. From that moment forward I told myself I would never leave her side; I would never give up on her or Sasha. Though, still I was frightened. In fact, that moment in time reminded me of the day I entered a hospital room and stood by my mother's side and told her, "I don't ever want to see dad like that again."

Later that night I went on my back patio and sat down in a rickety chair that could break at any moment, but I didn't care. Before heading to the patio, I took a beer from the fridge and unscrewed the bottle cap. I placed the beer bottle on the patio table and was suddenly overcome by emotion. I looked out into the night sky and ground my teeth nearly cracking them in half. I muttered up at the heaven's, "If you want to hurt someone, hurt me. Just leave my babies alone." From that moment forward both Sasha and Gabbie only incurred minor injuries and bruises along with common alignments such as a cold. It may be hard to believe but I think someone, God perhaps heard me that day?

Years later I would tell this very story to a close friend of mine. He asked me, "Did you ever think it was all just coincidence?" Rather than reply "no" I answered him with, "The way I see it is that there was no one else on planet earth who God saw fit to care for Sasha and Gabbie." He seemed confuse by this statement and replied, "You didn't answer my question." I smirked at him and said, "Yes, I did." To this day he still insists that I never gave him a truthful answer to his question. I keep telling him to "read between the lines."

When I finally went back inside, I sat on my couch and saw my girlfriend in the kitchen; she was getting a glass of water. She walked back into the living room where I was sitting and asked me, "Are you coming to bed?" I quickly replied, "In a minute I want to make sure Gabbie is okay." I watched Gabbie intently; I was mesmerized by her.; even inspired. I then heard my girlfriend ask, "What are you thinking about?" I looked up at her and asked her, "You really want to know?" She hesitated for a moment "Yea," she said. I sighed heavily and then mustered the courage to say what I should have said months prior, "I don't know if I love you anymore...," I felt the world suddenly fall off my shoulders and a wave of relief overcame me. "I told you Gabbie would be okay, but you didn't believe me; you lost faith in her and me." I lowered my head and then looked up at her while clenching my jaw tightly shut; I was furious. I spoke through my teeth and felt a strange power course through my exterminates. I snapped at her but refrained from yelling, "Didn't you?" I asked.

I stood there watching her; she seemed saddened but before she could speak, I blurted out, "Hell tried to break me, Hell tried to stop me..." I snarled, "and Hell failed." I clenched the muscles in my face and felt my blood boil; I wanted to yell but I didn't want to instigate a fight with her; I just wanted her to go and leave Sasha, Gabbie and I alone. Yet, I had to say something so I told her, "You're selfish." I look into her face to see that her eyes were empty as if she was dead. I then continued, "I can't love a selfish person."

She became angry and rolled her eyes then looked at me and told me she was tired and was going to go to bed. "Enough, Drew! " She turned and waved one hand at me. "Enough of your threats." I watched her for a few moments as she walked into the bedroom. She disappeared momentarily and then came back out into the living as if she had forgotten something. I wasn't looking at her when I heard her ask, "What is it about these dogs that you love so much?" I stood tall and then took a cigarette from behind my ear and placed it in the corner of my mouth; I had forgotten that it was there, but I acted as if I remembered. I clenched my fists at my sides as if I was preparing to fight. "What is it about these dogs that you don't love so much?" I asked her with an obnoxious tone of voice.

A few moments later the muscles in my arms and body began to relax. I light the cigarette dangling from my lips and then took a long, hard drag. She stood there staring at me; insulted that I was acting nonchalant. Finally, I spoke again. "I thought after all that we've been through you would have learned something?" She threw her arms out to her sides, "Oh, God! Here you go again!" She shouted at me. I shook my head side to side then walked to the coatrack at the front door and took my leather jacket off the hook and held it in one hand, "You will never know what the word love really means." I took another long drag on the cigarette then I blew smoke out of my mouth and continued saying, "To you it's just a word...," I paused and another long drag on my cigarette and then continued, saying, "to me it's a way of life; a pledge, a bond and a promise to never leave, never abandon and, even, if I must, die for who I love, including them - Sasha and Gabbie."

I turned around and headed to the door. She yelled at me almost instantly, "Don't walk away from me!" I put on my jacket and turned slightly over my shoulder and glanced down to Sasha and Gabbie and smiled reassuringly, "This isn't me walking away from you." A strange energy pulsed throughout my body. "This is me leaving you," I told her. I opened the door wide and looked back at her one last time, "As a matter of fact this is us leaving you." She stood there awe struck. A few moments later she raised her arm and flashed her middle finger at me. I laughed at her; mocking her weak attempt at trying to enrage me further. "You're no better than the rest of them." I told her while trying to be insulting at the same time. She quickly turned around and walked back to the bedroom and then she suddenly stopped. I took a few steps forward as if I was following her even though I wasn't; I just wanted to make sure she heard what I was going to say next. "All you had to do was believe in me; believe in our family." She stormed out of the bedroom and yelled, "What's to believe in?" I scoffed and replied, "My point exactly." She said nothing in response.

After a few minutes of waiting I then made one last attempt to try and get her to understand what I hoped she would have learned by now, "The sad truth is that I waited for you; I loved you even when I hated you, and all you could do was push me aside like a piece of garbage. Why? Because I hurt you?! Because

I love them more then you?" She looked at me with tears forming in her eyes; I hurt her feelings and she wanted to cry but I knew she wouldn't, not in front me. I unleashed my anger and shouted at the top of my lungs while pounding on my chest with a closed fist, "What about my hurt?! What about my pain?!" I breathed heavy for a few moments and then shouted even louder, "What about them?!" She reached out and tried to caress my hand, but I yanked my arm back, "My dogs are part of me; part of my soul and I am part of my dogs." She stepped back and we locked eyes. "Why can't you see that I can love you just as much as I can love them?" She interrupted me, "Drew..." However, I talked over her and continued saying, "We're leaving."

I scoffed and waved goodbye to her then muttered under my breath, "You ignorant motherfucker!" Even though my voice was faint she heard me and quickly retaliated with, "How dare you call me that!" I shrugged my shoulders and said, "I could call you much worse, you know?" She then tried to hurt my feelings and telling me what I already knew, "You're no saint yourself, ya know?" I acted smug and told her calmly, "I know what I am. However, you continue to fake what you will never be." I then took a step towards the front door. I guess something I said struck a nerve because I then watched her cup her face in her hands "I'm sorry," she told me. Moments later, she began to sob.

I trampled across the floor hurrying to the front door; her behavior was childish and offensive, and I wasn't going to tolerate it. I was finally going to leave. However, something pulled me back; it was a feeling I never felt before. I quickly turned around to face her and shouted, "Sorry!?" Her face was still buried in her hands as I heard her reply in a muffled voice, "I love you." I couldn't believe what I was hearing. I had a hard time knowing if this was another pathetic attempt at trying to manipulate me or if she was sincere; I wasn't going to fall for her games. "Look at them!" I yelled while pointing behind me to Sasha and Gabbie. "I said look!" She took her hands from her face and looked down at Sasha and Gabbie and then up at me. I demanded that she take responsibility for her actions; I wanted her to get a grip on a reality. I insisted and told her, "Don't tell me, tell them. Tell Sasha that you love her. As matter of fact hug Gabbie and tell her you love her too." I took off my jacket and smashed it onto the floor and screamed ferociously, "Show some fucking compassion for once in your life!"

It was at the very moment that something inside me snapped. As I bent forward to pick my jacket up off the floor, I heard her sniffle and then watched her carefully kneel down and call to Gabbie, and with fake smile on her face she attempted to coax Sasha to her as well. Yet, something surged through my body and I shouted louder than I ever shouted before; the sound of my voice shook the walls and rattled the windows, "Get away from them!" My footsteps echoed around me as I pounded across the floor rushing forward; I even looked back to see if there were imprints in the ground behind me. She stood up quickly as if someone or something yanked her up from the floor.

She slowly walked forward across the carpet being careful not to startle me. She stood in front of me and said, "It's incredible how much you love them." She then placed her arms around me and hugged me tight. "I think I understand now." I said nothing. She continued, "I'm sorry for hurting you." However, I refused to hug her back; my arms were limp at my sides. She let go of me and I stepped back; I could hear her heartbeat quicken in pace; she was becoming nervous. I walked backwards while continuing to look into her eyes and all the while remained quiet. She called my name, "Drew?" I could hear the worry in her voice as I turned and approached the couch. She stepped forward but stopped abruptly after just two steps. Her voice cracked as she asked me, "What are you doing?"

I leaned forward and picked up the ashtray from off the coffee table. While holding it in one hand turned it upside down and spilled the extinguished cigarette butts on the marble tabletop. I the place date ashtray back down and then turned around to face her. I could see the fear in her eyes; I knew that at any moment she could rush to get her cell phone for the bedroom and call the police, but I didn't care. I took the pack of cigarettes from my jacket pocket and opened it and placed a cigarette in my mouth. I lifted the lighter up in front of me and watched her out of the corner of my eye making sure she wasn't trying to sneak up on me. As I light the cigarette I said, "One day I will write a book about them." I paused momentarily and pointed at Sasha and Gabbie. I then continued telling her, "Their story will inspire people..." She interjected and told me with a smile on her face (I didn't know if she was genuinely happy or just faking it). "I hope you do write about them..." I walked towards her while exhaling smoke through my nostrils, "Their story will help people..." I stopped then flicked ash onto the pristine white carpet which she meticulously cleaned earlier that day. "Maybe I will even write about you too?"

Suddenly, she became stricken with fear and all expression fell from her face. "Are you okay?" She asked me with fright in her voice. "You're scaring me." I roared with laughter, "Me?" I took a drag on my cigarette which was burning down to the filter faster than I expected. "I'm fine. As a matter of fact I've never been better!" I then dropped the cigarette on the carpet and rubbed it out with my shoe. Her eyes widened and she jerked away from me as if she had just seen a spider crawl across the floor. I stepped forward and she squirmed like a worm caught on a lure. I told her, "You lost. I won't break." She refused to speak and didn't want to look at me. I then told her, "All this time you have been trying to get me to choose." I paused momentarily and glanced back to Sasha and Gabbie. I then said while turning back to face her, "Well, I made my choice."

I then stepped closer to her and she immediately retreated backward. She wasn't looking where she was going and tripped and fell to her hands and knees. She stood up quickly and grasped one wrist tight; she appeared to be in pain from the fall. I looked into her eyes and could tell she was frightened; my demeanor had suddenly gone from Jekyll to Hyde. I told her, "These are not just dogs. These are my daughters. And don't you ever forget that." She began to sob, and her voice cracked as she asked me, "Why are you acting like this?" I smiled sadistically and replied, "I already told you - because I love them."

"If you don't own a dog, at least one, there is not necessarily anything wrong with you, but there may be something wrong with your life."

- Roger A. Caras

CHAPTER ELEVEN
IT'S ME OR THE DOGS

Months had gone by since my psychotic break (as many people later called) and I was unsure of whether I wanted to leave or stay. Again, I attempted to reconcile with my girlfriend but quickly came to find out that my instincts were right after all. I realized not long after that I should have left when I had the chance. Yet, everyone has a breaking point and I was about to reach mine.

The sun had just set, and it was nearing 9pm. It was bitterly cold, and the weather report predicted snow and freezing rain in the overnight hours. Luckily for me I was considered by my peers to be a Polar Bear. More often than not people would remark, "Bro, you're not wearing socks!" I would look at them and factiously reply, "And?" Their eyes would widen and they would say, "There's two feet of snow on the ground!" As I walked away, I would shrug my shoulders while and often times hear myself calling out, "Really? I hadn't noticed." As you could imagine people would stare at me with a look of amazement and confusion.

As the night became colder and the threat of a wintery mix of snow and ice loomed over the small town, I was residing in something inside me erupted. Without hesitation I finally said to her (my girlfriend) what I should have said months earlier, if not years prior, "You can talk shit about me all you want, but you will not point blame at my dogs!" In all truthfulness I don't know what came over me that night. Anyone who knows me will tell you it takes a lot to push me to the point that I will become verbally aggressive. In retrospect I was probably being unfair but then again, I probably wasn't.

I charged into the bedroom without a word and began to pack my belongings. "Where are you going to go, huh?" She said to me with a smirk on her face. "It's the dead of winter. You'll freeze to death." I looked at her while stuffing a pair of shorts into my backpack. "I have a car, don't I?" She chuckled and replied, "You're telling me your gonna sleep in your car with two dogs? You must be kidding?" I hesitated for a moment and then replied, "Who ever said I would sleep?" She then began to realize that I was leaving and not coming back. "You'll be back..." She patronized me (which she knew I hated). "It's your apartment after all." I walked past her and said nothing only ground my teeth as I entered into the kitchen.

I took my coffee mug from out of the dishwasher and then began to make coffee. I could feel her eyes burning into the back of my skull; I knew she was staring at me from behind. "Drew," she said softly. "I guess I was right, wasn't I?" I gently placed my mug on the kitchen counter and replied, "Right about what?" She pulled out a chair from underneath the dinner table and sat down. "You do love them more than you love me." The coffee began to percolate. I shook my head and replied, "I can't believe how selfish you are." I then picked up my coffee mug (which was made of plastic) and turned around and threw it into the kitchen sink. It bounced up and into the air then spun widely across the room and fell the ground and landed with a soft thud. She jumped from her seat and shouted, "What is wrong with you?!" I walked to the coffee mug and picked it up and replied, "I was about to ask you the same question." I don't know why I threw the coffee mug at the sink. Maybe I was just frustrated or maybe I was just fed up? Or maybe it was both?

She stared at me and I was overcome with a sinking feeling that she thought I would throw the mug at her next. However, I would never do such a thing. I walked back to the coffee pot and began to pour coffee into the mug. I wanted to have a mature conversation with her but found myself repeating the same old rhetoric I always did. "You know the difference between me and you?" I asked her rhetorically. She said nothing as she sat back down in the chair. "I'll take that as a no," I said to her while tipping the sugar bowl into the coffee. She blurted out, "Drew, don't do this again." I stirred the sugar to dissolve it into the hot coffee then lifted the mug and took a sip then asked, "Do what?" She scoffed and replied, "This ridiculous debate about what love really is." Again, I sipped my coffee. "Whatever, you need to hear it!" I insisted while demanding that she listen to what I had to say. "I know what love is..." I thought she was going to interrupt me, so I paused and waited for some kind of childish remark. However, she refrained from speaking so I continued, "It's here in this room at this very moment yet you yet keep your eyes shut to the truth because even now you are stubborn and hardheaded." She laughed and asked me, "Where do you come up that with corny shit?"

I turned to face the cabinets on the wall behind me. I placed my coffee mug down on the counter underneath the cupboards and lowered my head and stared intently at my feet. "I don't know what you want from me anymore but this bullshit..." I paused then turned looked at her from over my shoulder. "I'm done!" Again, she continued to insult me and called my remarks "corny", "stupid" and, even, "childish."

A few moments passed until I picked up my coffee mug and walked over to the sink then placed the mug down next to me and turned on the fact. I washed my hands in the luke warn water then dried them with a kitten towel that was hanging over the handle of the stove. I then leaned back against the countertop behind me and crossed my arms in front of my chest. I told her, "You see, you have love, a multitude of love as a matter of fact and yet can't even see it even when it's staring you dead in the face." She ran one hand through her hair, "Drew, that's not the point." I walked to the edge of the kitchen counter and replied, "That's exactly the point!" I said while pointing at her. Still, she refused to listen to reason. "One day you'll figure out my riddles but until then you will continue to deny the truth." She looked at me from out of the corner of one eye. "You want me to call your bluff? Is that it?" She asked me in a defiant tone of voice.

I said nothing and walked back into the bedroom. As I stood in the bedroom packing my backpack, I heard her call my name, "Drew?" I continued to put clothes into the backpack and again she called out, "Drew, don't ignore me." I zipped up the backpack and called for Sasha and Gabbie. I took their leashes out of the closet and put them around my neck and then told them to go to the front door. As I walked past her, I said, "My fate will be no different from theirs." I opened the door and Sasha ran out (but, she stopped a few feet in front of me and then turned around fully and waited patiently for me). Gabbie, however, stood next to me waiting for me to lead her outside.

I pet Gabbie on the top of her head and looked back over my shoulder. I stared at my girlfriend for a few seconds before saying, "If you can't see it by now you never will." I then began to walk to Sasha and waved Gabbie outside. I heard my girlfriend call to me and ask, "See what?" I focused on Sasha then trend slightly to see Gabbie directly behind me. I then replied,

"That they love you just as much as I do." I quickly directed my attention back to Sasha and Gabbie. I then looked back and continued to say, "I see now that you won't ever allow me to be happy." I paused momentarily and whistled to Sasha; she was straying too far from the house. I then looked back at the doorway where my girlfriend stood and said with conviction in my voice, "I won't be like you." Then, from seemingly out of nowhere a burst of anger overcame me, "I won't be weak!" I shouted.

After a few moments I calmed down and exhaled a heavy breath and told her, "I hope one day that you will be able to see that love is all you need; not money, cars, nice houses, and stupid shit like that..." She interrupted me and asked me sarcastically, "Didn't John Lennon say that?" I smirked while asking her factiously, "Are you saying he was wrong?" She scoffed and put her hands on her hips and bite her bottom lip, "Drew, it's late and you're emotional...," She waited for me to respond but I refused to get dragged into an argument. She continued, saying, "Why don't you come inside, and we can talk?" I felt insulted; manipulated almost. I lashed out and yelled at her, "Talk?!" I calmly turned to Sasha and Gabbie and told them to sit and wait. The blood in my veins rushed to my face and I yelled, "I tried to talk to you for years, but you didn't listen!" The force of my voice made the night air momentarily come to a halt.

A light in a neighboring building suddenly came on and I saw a silhouette of a woman at the window; she peeked through the blinds and was carefully investigating what was going on outside. My girlfriend retreated into the house and shielded herself behind the door. I stomped across the concrete and then suddenly stopped when I heard Sasha whine. I looked back at Sasha and smiled, "It's okay, Sash." I turned away from the apartment door and walked up beside Sasha and Gabbie. Sasha spun in circles while Gabbie jumped up on me. I laughed and pet both of them simultaneously.

I looked back at the apartment door to see my girlfriend standing in the doorway. "All you had to do was have faith, to fight and stand with me even when we were losing. That's all I needed from you. My only regret is that you refuse to see past today. I know things will be hard for me but as long as I have them..." I pointed to Sasha and Gabbie then continued, "In the end I will win." I then began to walk to my car while leading Sasha and Gabbie on their leashes. I stopped and turned slightly and looked back over my shoulder. While shivering and trying not to show it I told her, "No matter what I will never leave them. I will never abandon them. I will never give up because things become hard. I may face defeat, but I will show you, and the world that my failures are in fact victories; I will only become stronger. That is what make me better than you...." I paused; a chill ran down my spine. I was overcome by a premonition; a vision which flashed before my eyes but was gone only moments later. The felling was intense, but I was unable to recall what I had just seen.

It was then that she opened her mouth readying a rhetoric of obnoxious slander, but I interjected and continued, saying, "You have no faith in me, no faith in my daughters..." I paused and stared into her eyes, "Or yourself." She frantically reached forward with one arm, but I was too far for her to grab me. Her voice cracked as she shouted hysterically, "Drew, quit the bullshit! You know I love you!" I stopped dead in my tracks and dropped my chin to my chest then looked at Sasha then to Gabbie and smiled reassuringly My girlfriend pleaded with me and shouted, "Come back, please!"

I wasted no time and turned around quickly then pumped one fist out in front of me and shouted, "You are a coward!" She ignored me completely and replied, "I love you, please, don't leave!" I stared into her eyes and ground my teeth, "My fate will be no different than theirs." Seconds later, she became hostile and shouted, "Fuck you!" I shook my head and laughed and said without looking at her, "Love and happiness is something you will never understand." She felt compelled to retaliate with harsh words, "Yea, well, you're an asshole. You know that?"

I turned around and clenched the muscles in my jaw tightly shut. I pointed at her but quickly lowered my arm and bite my bottom lip to keep myself from saying something I would regret. I walked backwards while staring at her and all the while shook my head in disgust. As I neared the car I turned around and quickly opened the driver's side passenger's door. Immediately Sasha jumped in followed by Gabbie. I gently closed the door being careful not to catch either of their tails in the door jam. I turned to face front and a moment later opened the driver's door and sat in the seat and started the ignition. I lowered the window of my Dodge Charger and looked at her for a few moments while she stood motionless in the doorway of the apartment shaking uncontrollably from the freezing cold. I put the gear shift in drive and then said, "Don't ever say I didn't try." She shouted at me, "Just leave already!" I then revved the engine of the car and sped away like a bat out of Hell down the dimly light street which lead to the main road.

I raced to the entrance of the highway and headed south on I-95 towards New York. I got to my parents' house a few hours later. They had no idea I was even there. When they awoke the next morning, they were shocked to see Sasha, Gabbie and I eating breakfast in the kitchen. I told my father what had happened and that I was leaving New York for a job in Cleveland. He said nothing only nodded his head signaling to me that he agreed me with my decision. A few hours later I changed my phone number, closed my Facebook, set up a new email account and disappeared from the face of the earth...

...and I never saw her again.

PSALM 4

Answer me when I call to you, my righteous God.
Give me relief from my distress; have mercy
on me and hear my prayer.

How long will you people turn my glory into shame?
How long will you love delusions and seek false
gods?

Know that the LORD has set apart his faithful servant
for himself; the LORD hears when I call to him.

Tremble and do not sin; when you are on your beds,
search your hearts and be silent.

Offer the sacrifices of the righteous and trust in the
LORD. 6 Many, LORD, are asking, "Who will bring
us prosperity?" Let the light of your face shine
on us. Fill my heart with joy when their grain
and new wine abound.

In peace I will lie down and sleep, for you alone,
LORD, make me dwell in safety.

"An open mind and helpful hands can do much to change a dog's future."

\- Mary Debono

CHAPTER TWELVE
DAY OF RUIN

PT. 1
THE WILL OF GOD

There's an old saying that goes, "Always expect the unexpected." Still, who could have ever expected what would happen next? It had been nearly five years since that explosive night where I once and for all broke the cycle of negativity which infected my life for so long; the night when I sped away in my car and headed back to New York hoping to start my life over. However, starting over would mean that I would first have to endure heartache after heartache, and it would all begin in Flushing, New York.

Let me say that at this point I was completely unaware that anything was wrong with me physically (emotionally is a whole other story). I came to realize in a short amount of time that the people who I thought loved me and cared about my well-being had suddenly turned their backs on me; cherishing material things more than extending a helping hand to someone who was in dire need of assistance. Recently, I met someone who told me, "People are made to disappoint you." This person was right, of course. Though, I cannot say this about everyone, however. My father who had every right to let me rot in misery came to my aid when no one else would. I owe him more than I could every repay him.

Okay, back to my story. I was living in a hotel; the reasons why are unimportant. Of course, Sasha and Gabbie were with me (by now you should know that I wouldn't go anywhere without them). For so long it had been one disappointment after another. I had no money (very little actually), no car, no home and no future...or so it seemed.

As each day came and went all I could think about was protecting Sasha and Gabbie and staying positive even when there was nothing to stay positive about. I tried desperately to keep food available for Sasha and Gabbie; resorting to anything and everything to make sure they didn't starve even though it was inevitable I would. I walked for over two miles in each direction just to go to a store that sold cheap dog food; it wasn't the best, but it was better than nothing.

Finally, a week before Christmas in December of 2014 I caught a break...or so I thought. Before I continue let me say that it is incredibly hard to describe to you, the reader the feeling of not only hopelessness but helplessness as well, and the effects such feelings take on a person's mind and body. Yet, unlike the homeless man you see on the street corner who remains pinned down by his plight I had a plan; a plan that only one year later would take me on the greatest adventure of my life, and bring me over three thousand miles away from the city I knew best - New York.

Even though I had the determination of Bull I was telling myself to give up, however. So many times, I thought it would be better for me to surrender Sasha and Gabbie to a family (or shelter) that could care for them. However, with each thought I heard a voice of a young girl echo in my head who once told me, "Without you they (Sasha and Gabbie) would wither and die. I've said it more than once in this book and I will say it again - as long as I was alive, I wasn't going to let that happen. Very few people knew how bad my life had become; even my own family was oblivious to the truth. Blame? Well, no, I'm not blaming anyone other than myself.

Before continuing let me repeat what a close friend of mine told me, "It is a fact that our thoughts determine our existence." However, my thoughts were now betraying me. Sadly, like most people I refused to believe that simply by thinking it my life would change for the better. Even while experiencing so many awful nights where sorrow compelled me to think and act irrationally, I never once thought that all I had to do to change my fate was to think I could, and unbeknownst to me by thinking negative thoughts I was digging my own grave.

From here on forward this chapter of my story will be both alarming and frightening. You will say, "My God!" and, even, at times exclaim, "You should be dead, Drew!" Why should I be dead? Well, you see with all my sacrifices; the long and tiring walks, lack of sleep, stress and paranoia, little to no food, and only coffee and cigarettes to keep me warm I was slowly dying, and I never even knew it...until it was too late, that is.

As I said earlier, I caught a break. It was one day while sitting in the hotel room and tirelessly searching for a one-bedroom apartment I finally found what I was looking for (it was the apartment I mentioned earlier which was located in Flushing, New York). It was too easy to find, and I should have known things were only going to end bad. However, I was a desperate and desperate times call for desperate measures. Right? Less than twenty-four hours later I was out of the hotel and into the new apartment. I was relieved to say the least. Yet, the relief I felt would be short lived.

Three weeks later and only a few days after Christmas but before New Year's I would collapse and momentarily black out. As I awoke, I came to realize that I was no longer able to stand up without falling down, walk without hitting a wall, sleep without vomiting or even eat or drink. As the days came and went it became increasingly obvious that I was on the verge of a serious health risk (I would later find out it was something called extreme dehydration and vertigo). To make matters worse my blood pressure was dangerously high and increasing rapidly, and even my stress level was considered by the doctor to be, "life threatening."

For two weeks I laid in bed drinking a small amount of water every few days and eating pancakes and waffles which I had delivered from a nearby diner that my roommate at the time so graciously paid for. One evening in-particular was worse than any other. In fact, this is the day that I called my father and told him goodbye and that I loved him dearly. That evening I was certain I was going to die.

As dusk approached, I was overcome by a strange feeling. Many people know what nausea feels like, correct? However, have you ever just vomited without any prior warning or feeling of any kind? I recall laying on my bed and looking through the window; the shades were up, and I could see over the rooftop of the adjacent building. I remember burping first and then the room began to spin. Next, I simply passed out.

About an hour later I awoke and to my surprise I was on the floor; I must have rolled off the bed in my sleep. As I looked around the room, I heard Sasha begin to whine; she was laying on my legs with her head across my thighs and looking up at me. I had double vision and all I could see was a hazy blur in front of me. Though, I knew it was Sasha who was onto of me; Gabbie was lying on the bed with her head hanging over the edge staring down at me; she was watching me meticulously. I called to Sasha, "Sash, what's wrong girl?" I asked. I lifted my head which felt like it weighed a ton. I raised one hand to my forehead and rubbed my skull. I gently shut my eyes but as I opened them, I could see nothing but black; I had become temporarily blind (or so I hoped).

Sasha shifted her weighed as I tried to get up and I struggled immensely to do so. I could hear whining all around me and then a loud bark (which came from Gabbie on the bed) startled me. I somehow found a way to get up but as I began to step forward on the hardwood floor I collapsed to my hands and knees. I fluttered my eye lids but still I couldn't see anything but darkness.

I crawled slowly at first to the side of the room where I thought the door was; I was trying to get help from my roommate. Yet, as I got closer to the door vomit spewed from my mouth and across the room and onto a pile of clothes which had been laying on the floor for over two weeks; in my state I was unable to wash them. Suddenly, my eyesight returned, and I looked back over my shoulder to Sasha and Gabbie. Sasha came up off the floor slightly, but I called to her and said, "I'm okay, Sash. Stay, girl, stay." However, things worsened only moments later.

I heaved again but this time blood and vomit came up; but more blood then vomit actually. I looked down onto the clothes and saw blotches of red. At first, I didn't think it was blood, but it was obvious only moments later it was. Then a thought rushed through my head and I questioned if I could be bleeding internally? What would have caused such a thing to happen? I threw up another two times onto the clothes; a mixture of blood and bile and when it was over, I was too weak to move.

A minute or so passed and I watched as Gabbie began to slide off the bed like she always does but at a quicker pace than usual; I got the feeling she was trying to help me in some way? I called out and told her to stay and reassured her that I was okay even though she knew otherwise. I laid on the floor and struggled to breathe and every so often I would stare up at the ceiling, and then occasionally glance over to Sasha and Gabbie and saw that they were watching me intently; I don't think either one of them ever blinked. I slept on the floor for the rest of the night because I was too afraid to move. I'm not sure how many times I blacked out, but it must have been at least a half a dozen times.

I awoke the next morning to the sun gleaming in my face. The rays of light were warm on my skin and I felt like I was being watched (even though I was the only human being within earshot). I felt better but still I had a hard time standing and walking. However, I was determined to fight through whatever sickness was overtaking my body. I began to get dressed and took off the clothes I had on (which were stained from vomit) and tossed them onto the pile tucked away in the corner near the door. Suddenly, my phone rang; it was my father. I answered the phone and pretended that nothing was wrong. "How you feeling?" He asked. I buckled my belt and secured my jeans, "Feeling better..." He then quickly asked, "Are you eating?" I assured him that I was. I replied, "Yea, just had some eggs actually." I reached for the bedroom door and heard him say, "You need to get a job. You gotta live within your means. You understand what that means? You're not Diamond Jim Brady, got it?" I rolled my eyes and replied, "I know, dad, and I am..." I coughed then continued, "I will, I mean." We hung up and I turned my focus to Sasha and Gabbie and asked them, "This must be karma, huh, girls?"

I didn't want to tell my father that I was still suffering from some kind of fatal sickness (or at least it felt that way) and vomiting occasionally as well as having a hard time breathing or even standing for that matter. He was worried about me enough and to put him through any more pain would have crushed me completely. I opened the bedroom door and I felt a tingling feeling shoot through my hand. I ignored it at first and continued walking slowly over to the stairs; I was going to go outside and get some fresh air. I thought that by going outside and spending time in the cold it would help me in some way? However, I couldn't have been more wrong.

I began to shimmy my way to the staircase and when I got near it, I placed my hand on the railing. Suddenly, I felt the tingling feeling again surge through my hand and just like before I lost my ability to see. I stood there hoping that my vision would return quickly and as I did, I could feel everything around me begin to spin uncontrollably. I turned back and tripped over my feet as I tried to get back into my bedroom. I fell completely face first onto the floor; smashing against the tile with no way to brace myself; at first, I thought I was falling down the stairs.

Hearing the loud crash Sasha came out of the room and poked her nose into my face; I guess it was her way of telling me she was there in front of me. It hurt to smile but I did so anyway and told her, "No matter what happens to me, Sash, you and Gabs will be okay." My skin began to get hot and it felt like I was on fire. A few moments passed and my breathing became suddenly sporadic, "I will make sure you never alone." I told her and then couched. I struggled through somehow mustered all my might and lifted myself off the floor and sat upright against the wall. I sat there breathing heavily while holding one hand against my chest and thinking if I should call an ambulance?

My vision returned moments later, and I looked at Sasha; in her eyes I saw worry. We stared into each other eyes for a few moments and then I pulled her close with one arm and kissed her on the top of her head and said in a heavy breath, "It's me, you and Gabs forever, girl." Then, almost immediately my chest constricted, and my muscles tightened; my arms and legs froze from the immense strain shooting through my body. I spoke through my teeth while trying not to panic and called out to Sasha, "It's us
three forever, Sash." I heaved heavy then told her, "I love you."

Sasha began to whimper and paced from side to side. I knew she was worried but there was little I could do to calm her down. In some ways I thought that perhaps her barking would alert a neighbor to the fact that something was terribly wrong. However, begin that I was in New York the odds of help coming were slim to none. New York is an unforgiving city and the people are even more laxed in their concern for someone else well-being. I was certain that Sasha's loud barking would go unnoticed by the neighbors.

It was no surprise, however that Gabbie was also concerned about the strange behavior I was exhibiting. A few minutes later, Gabbie began barking and even found her way out into the hallway where she stood looking at me and Sasha while trying to conclude if we were playing or if something more serious was occurring.

I fluttered my eyelids and smiled at Gabbie then called her over to me. She obeyed my command and came to my side and then laid down next to me. She rolled over onto her back and wanted me to pet her belly. I laughed but my laughter quickly became a hacking couch. "I'm sorry, Gabs. I can't play right now," I told her. She then rolled back over onto her stomach and looked at me while smiling; her tongue was dangling out of the side of her mouth. I reached forward and pet her on the top of her head and told her I loved her. I asked both Sasha and Gabbie to back into the bedroom. Gabbie ignored me completely while Sasha went back into the room. Yet, Sasha had no intention on staying. After a few seconds she came barreling out of the room with her squeaky ball in her mouth. I laughed; she was adorable. However, the pain in the skull was getting worse. I cringed my eyes and clenched my jaw shut. I struggled to talk but somehow found a way to speak. "Stay," I said. I then slouched over to one side; my vision was becoming foggy. Then, my body went limp. A few seconds later I fell over onto the floor and could no longer see.

Sasha began to whimper and Gabbie made a sound I never heard before. Sadly, I had no strength left in me and allowed my body to succumb to the pain. I was unable to talk, see, and, even, breath. My chest was constricting worse than last time. A strange tingling feeling began to course though my left arm and my fingertips went numb. Then, I simply passed out.

PSALM 32

Have mercy on me, my God, have mercy on me, for
in you I take refuge. I will take refuge in the
shadow of your wings until the disaster
has passed.

I cry out to God Most High, to God, who
vindicates me.

He sends from heaven and saves me, rebuking
those who hotly pursue me—God sends
forth his love and his
faithfulness.

I am in the midst of lions; I am forced to dwell
among ravenous beasts— men whose teeth
are spears and arrows, whose tongues
are sharp swords.

Be exalted, O God, above the heavens; let
your glory be over all the earth.

"If you pick up a starving dog and make prosperous, he will not bite you. This is the principal difference between a dog and man."

- Mark Twain

CHAPTER THIRTEEN
DAY OF RUIN

PT. 2
THE HAND OF GOD

All I remember was hearing my roommate shout my name as she came rushing up to the top landing of the staircase. My eyelids sprung open, but my eyes were unable to focus on what was in front of me. My roommate kneeled down in front of me (at least I thought she did) and stared into my face then placed one hand on my shoulder and asked me what was wrong. I shrugged her hand off my shoulder and then heard Sasha whine from the bedroom. She yelled back at Sasha and I lashed out and pushed her backwards, "Don't yell at her!" I lifted myself up off the ground and stumbled only once as I entered my bedroom. I could barely see but recognized Sasha and called out to her and said, "She didn't mean it, girl." I then apologized to my roommate for shouting at her and then asked her politely to leave me alone and excused myself into my bedroom.

To my dismay my roommate refused to leave and insisted that I get help, but I adamantly declined. "Drew," she said. "Now, you're just being stupid." I laughed and planked myself down onto the soft mattress of the bed. Moments later Sasha jumped up and laid down at the foot of the bed. I tried not to collapse my weight on top of Gabbie (who was lying on my pillow at the head of the bed). I laid my head down onto my pillow and shut my eyes. "I'm fine," I said while covering my eyes with one hand.

I knew she was staring at me; I could feel her looking me up and down. I opened my eyes slightly and squinted; I was annoyed and just wanted her to leave. She stepped further into the bedroom and said, "No, you're not fine, Drew." She looked to the nightstand bedside the bed where a dozen empty coffee cups (possible more) were scattered in no particular order. "Did you drink all these today?" She asked inquisitively. I sat upright and placed my elbow on the bed to support my weight then squinted my eyes, "Actually, those are from last night and this morning..." She interrupted me, "Did you eat?" I sighed heavy and shook my head, "What are you? My mother?" She scoffed and I continued, saying, "Please just leave."

A few seconds passed and I heard her begin to press buttons on her cell phone (an iPhone, I believe).

I sat completely up, "Who you calling?" I asked her but she didn't answer me. "Are you deaf? I'm not your problem!" I yelled at her ferociously; now she was beginning to piss me off. I then heard her begin to talk into the phone, "Hi. Yes, can you please send an ambulance..." I shouted again, "Hang up the phone!" She left the room out of fear that I would try and grab the phone from her hand. She slammed the door and the sound reverted back and forth in my skull. I clenched my eyes tightly shut.

Her voice was faint, but I could hear her giving the street address to the 911 operator. I stood up and stumbled forward then swayed side to side until I finally crashed up against the wall next to me. I knocked over a small lap that I found in the garage a few days earlier; it had no lamp shade. The sound of me falling must have startled her and she came rushing back into the room. She gently grabbed me by one arm and lead me to the bed and told me to lie down and that the ambulance would soon arrive. I shrugged my shoulders and again insisted she leave. Again, she refused.

I lied in bed trying as hard as I could to keep my eyes open; I was overcome by the sensation of vertigo. A few seconds later I jolted upright and heaved blood over the side of the bed. She jerked away from me; her face was twisted, and her expression was morbid. "Drew," she said. "This is serious!" I chuckled once then replied, "No shit, Sherlock!" She then looked down at her phone as if she was expecting a call, but I realized she was only checking the time. "What's wrong with you?" She asked me with a tone of anger. "I'm sick. Duh!" She scoffed at my factious remark and replied, "That much is obvious." I looked up at her and leaned forward then placed one hand on my thigh to support my weight; my body felt weak and lethargic. "Why do you hate life, Drew? Do you want to die? Is that it?" She asked me in a brazen voice. I looked to Sasha and Gabbie, "Hate is a strong word." I told her. She thrust her arms downward at her sides and replied, "Then get the fuck up and let me drive you to the hospital."

I was finally cooperating or so she thought. She watched me as I stood up and wobbled from side to side. She then said happily, "It's about time." I hobbled to the nightstand and opened the small draw then took out an unopened pack of cigarettes. I fell back on to the bed and unwrapped the cigarettes then took one from the pack and placed in my mouth. She scorned me with her eyes while calling me names including, "idiot," "dumbass," and "moron."

I smoked my cigarette and listened to her verbally attack me with one derogatory remark after another. I rolled my eyes and hoped she would just stop talking when I suddenly heard the doorbell ring. She became overly excited and shouted, "They're here!" I insisted, "I'm not going." She grabbed me by one arm and said, "Yes, you are!" She yanked me forward off the bed with immense strength. I wanted to fight back and push her away from me, but I was too weak. Just then my body went limp and I lost control of my legs; my knees buckled, and I collapsed to the floor. Thankfully, she held me tight to keep me from crashing to the ground and hurting myself. She cried out, "Drew!" I tried to speak but I as I did, I again vomited blood.

A voice called from downstairs; it was her boyfriend. "Babe?" He called out. She quickly replied, "Up here!" I smirked and looked up at her from over my shoulder, "It's not the ambulance, is it?" She looked down at me while yelling to her boyfriend, "Help me!" Suddenly, I collapsed onto my stomach and the room began to spin. "Babe, hurry!" She shouted. Almost immediately I heard footsteps trample up the stairs and the bedroom door creak open.

My roommate's boyfriend stood over me. I heard him ask, "Is he alright?" My roommate was panic stricken, and her voice was tearful as she replied, "I think he's dead!" Though, I wasn't dead or unconscious...yet (even though it felt like I was). Though, I couldn't move or speak so I guess she figured I had subsumed to the sickness overcoming me? I grunted softly to let her know I was still breathing. Without speaking a word her boyfriend then lifted me off the ground and placed my arm around his shoulder and began to walk me out of the room. He said while hurrying to the stairs, "Let's go!" My roommate then closed the door behind her and I heard the door lock. I assumed she must have locked the room with the spare key. Or perhaps found mine and used my copy? I could barely speak but somehow found the strength to say, "Please don't leave them alone."

My roommate's boyfriend stopped and looked to the bedroom door. He then to my roommate and told her, "Stay with them. I'll take Drew to the ER." A claiming feeling overcame me as I then realized it was now safe to finally leave; I was confident that Sasha and Gabbie were in good hands. I then thanked my roommate for staying and watching over them and she promised me that nothing would happen to either one of them. She smiled at me and said, "They'll be here waiting for you when you come back." I graciously nodded to her. "Just get better, Drew, that's all." I then asked her in a heavy breath while holding back the erg to vomit, "Give them a lot of kisses, they deserve it." I coughed then continued, "And tell them to be good cause daddy's watching." She chuckled softly. I tried to stay in good sprints, but a cryptic feeling was overcoming me. I didn't want to admit it, but I was scared that that would be the last time I would ever see either one of them.

The next twenty minutes would be Hell indeed. I found myself lying in the backseat of a car. I couldn't remember how I got there, however? I assumed that I must have been placed there. Then I heard the car start and a voice say, "Drew, we'll be there soon, buddy." I hacked and replied, "I'll try not to vomit in your car." I then rolled my head to one side and buried my face in the seat cushion.

All I remember following that moment was waking up in a wheelchair and being rushed into the emergency room. I remember two sliding doors that opened like magic and someone asking me for my medical insurance card (which I didn't have either). Next, I heard a woman behind a counter say, "He needs to be seen immediately." She motioned for us follow her and moments later a man took control of the wheelchair and lead me behind a set of curtains. Next, I was lifted out of the wheelchair and placed onto an examination table where I waited for the inevitable.

PSLAM OF THE FUTURE

Thunder shows the disapproval of God: yet your
approval of Jesus was heard as thunder!

Does lightning mean you're angry with me: is
there still power in primitive ideas?

The forces around us can be frightening, however
caused: the earth has terrifying wonders to
shake us - the earthquake that unsettles
a mighty city: the eruption that rips
open the quiet mountainside.

No matter what we do to pollute our
planet: the forces inside it still change our world.

If the lava-flow can be home to life in a hundred
years: the earth may yet survive
the end of humanity.

Your time, our God, is far longer than ours: your
purposes don't depend only on me; why
should I think this day's work so vital?
Why do we feel that we're at the
center of time?

When we're as dead as the dinosaurs, you'll
be alive: if our experiment fails, you
could re-create your world.

"To sit with a dog on a hillside on a glorious afternoon is to be back in Eden, where doing nothing was not boring--it was peace."

- Milan Kundera

CHAPTERFOURTEEN
DAY OF RUIN

PT. 3
THE PATH OF GOD

I must have blacked out momentarily because a few minutes later I was jolted awake as my shirt was ripped open and suction cups were attached to my chest; I could see long cable running the length of the room which were plugged into monitors of all sorts; they were stuck to my chest, torso and head. As I laid still on the examination table my hearing was suddenly overwhelmed by beeping sounds which reverberated in my ears; it felt like torture of some sort. The constant tone of endless electronic sounds were more irritating then the sensation of vertigo which forced me to vomit every fifteen minutes.

Then, from seemingly out of nowhere a man leaned over me and shined a flashlight in my eyes; he was obviously a doctor. "Mr. Glick?" He asked me rhetorically. "Can you hear me?" I squinted my eyes and heard him ask again, "Mr. Glick? Do you know where you are?" I fluttered my eyes and when I opened them completely, I was staring into a blinding white light. To escape the light, I turned my head and quickly noticed a nurse beside me. I turned back to the doctor and lifted my hand to my face, but the doctor swatted it away. I tried to get up off the table, but he placed his palm on my chest and forced me back down. I glanced out of the corner of my eye and saw that the nurse was holding a syringe out on front of her in her right hand. I suddenly began to panic and started twisting and turning like a fish caught on a lure.

I kicked my legs and flailed my arms hitting anything I could; bed pans and medical instruments went flying in all directions and crashed loudly to the ground. The doctor yelled at me to calm down and waved at the nurse to leave the room. A few moments passed and the doctor removed his hand from my chest and stepped back and then asked me politely to sit up. I struggled for only a moment as I turned my body sideways and let me legs dangle off the edge of the table. The doctor then put his hands in his jacket pockets and stood in a relaxed position. "Mr. Glick," he said. "You're lucky to be alive." I scoffed and replied, "Luck has nothing to do with it." The doctor removed his hands from his pockets and turned to face a counter behind him. He said while looking at a Manilla folder on the counter, "I would argue the latter." I jumped off the table and landed flatfooted making a loud clapping noise on the cold tile. The sound startled the doctor and he turned abruptly around and told me to sit back down.

I looked around the small room for my clothes; I had forgotten then were ripped to pieces and probably in the incinerator. "I'd really appreciate it if you gave me my pants back," I told the doctor sarcastically. He said nothing as he turned back to the table and picked up a small manilla folder. He opened the folder and thumbed through the pages; some of the papers looked like charts. He then closed the folder and turned fully around and stared at me for what seemed like hours.

I was becoming impatient and finally blurted out, "Are we having a staring contest or something?" The doctors face turned grim. "Mr. Glick," he said to me while walking forward. "This is a very serious situation." I chuckled and said, "Tell me something I don't know." He seemed confused and asked, "If you know then why do you not care?" I looked at him and hesitated. I knew if I told him the truth, he would think I was crazy. I stood before him deep in thought then finally replied, "There's only two reasons why I am still walking this earth." I began to walk to the door of the room. "Thanks, Doc, I feel much better now," I said while trying to be funny. "But I have to go. I have to get home." He rushed to the door and grabbed me by my wrist and refused to let me leave. I glanced down at his hand and told him, "Please let go of me." He shook his head and replied, "I can't do that." I sighed heavy then crunched my eyes and batted my eyelids; my head was beginning to ache, and I felt like I was going to faint at any moment. "I know my rights," I smirked at him then continued and said, "We both know that I can leave whenever I want." He was dumbfounded; shocked almost. I then told him, "So, I will ask you again to please let go of me." I pulled at his hand, but he only tightened his grip.

A few minutes passed until the doctor reluctantly let go of me; I nodded in appreciation. As I turned the doorknob I listened as he told me, "Mr. Glick," he paused for a moment while waiting for me to turn back and look at him. "If you refuse treatment, I can assure you things will only worsen." I licked my my lips; I was thirsty and needed something to drink. I nodded my head signaling to him I understood. I then opened the door slightly and again I heard him call out, "You will either end up in a coma or die," he said to me in a cryptic tone of voice. "Is that what you want?" I let go of the doorknob and dropped my arm to my side. I turned and looked into his eyes and asked him, "Do you have children?" He seemed surprised by my question. "I have a daughter," he answered. I smiled warmly then replied, "I have two." I could tell by his expression that he didn't believe me. I didn't really care what he thought. I then continued, "That's why I have to go."

I began to think random thoughts of Sasha and Gabbie. The from out of nowhere I felt the sudden urge to cry but I forcefully held back the tears. "If I die," I told him confidently. "Then I die." He was appalled; sickened almost that I would say such a thing. I then felt a tingling sensation course through both of my hands. I lowered my head and held my hands out in front of me; my hands were shaking but I wasn't nervous. After a moment or two I lowered my hands and turned slightly and looked at the doctor, "All that matters are my babies, nothing else." I then quickly turned back to the door and reached for the doorknob while telling him, "Not even me." I sighed then took one last look over my shoulder back at him. A few moments later I felt my body getting weak and heavy and I knew had no time to waste.

I opened the door but this time the doctor said nothing. "Is he really letting me leave?" I thought. I walked forward exiting the room and out into the hallway. Almost immediately I was confronted by a security guard. "Sir," he said. "Go back to the room." He pointed behind me to the door. "The doctor has not released you from his care yet." I threw my arms out to my sides; I was fed up. "Holy fuck!" I shouted. "What's with you people?" I looked around pointing at random individuals; nurses and doctors who were attending to other patients. "I just want to go..." Then, everything went back and a loud thud was heard echoing down the hallway. I had collapsed and when I awoke, I found myself back on the cold aluminum table that I found myself on when I first arrived. However, this time I had restraints around my wrists and ankles; it was obvious that this time I wasn't going anywhere.

I heard the doctor speak. His voice was low and soft as he said, "Mr. Glick, this is for your own good." I jerked my arms up but with the restraints secured tightly around my wrists I was only able raise them about four inches off the table. I snarled at him as he continued, saying, "You need to calm down." I stared at him and watched his every move. "I'm fine!" I shouted. I felt a slight pinch a moment later and seconds later I had realized that I had stuck me with a needle. "This will help you calm down." I growled but the sedative he injected in me was quickly taking effect; I felt a calling peace overcome me. "There we are," said the doctor. "Now," he cleared his throat. "Tell me again why you want to leave." I rolled my eyes at him. "I promised them, that's why." He looked at me inquisitively. "Who's them?" He asked. Again, I rolled my eyes. I was becoming frustrated with his intrusive questions. "My daughters," I told him. He said nothing and all I could hear was the buzzing of the florescent lights above me. "You seem a little young to have children." I sighed as I then realized I had no choice but to indulge him in a useless conversation. I smirked and replied, "Looks can be deceiving."

After a few minutes of our pointless conversation the doctor unbuckled the restraints binding my wrists and ankles. I sat up and asked him, "So..." I rubbed one wrist with my opposite hand and continued, "What's the verdict?" The doctor stood in front of me and began to tell me the bad news. "Well," he said. "You're incredibly dehydrated." I interrupted him and jokingly said, "Oh, that's not good, is it?" He sighed and then continued, "The bad news is that you are also suffering from vertigo." I placed my hands on my knees and blurted out, "No shit!" I snapped my fingers, "I really thought I was just dizzy."

The doctor was angry at my sarcastic remarks and insisted I be quiet and listen. "Mr. Glick," he said while he reached to the wall and took down a clipboard. "We are going to need to admit you." He then took a pen from his front coat pocket and handed me the clip board and pen. I jolted back and asked him, "What's this?" He pushed the clipboard forward and replied, "We need some further information or..." I jumped off the table and swung one arm out in front of me. "No fucking way!" I told him. With an empty expression on his face he took the papers from the clipboard then placed the clipboard down at his side and crumpled up the papers. A moment later he tossed the papers in the waste basket trying to mock Michael Jordan and said, "I knew you were going to say that." He placed the pen back in his jacket pocket and said, "Then, I have no choice but to let you leave." I was overcome with relief and shouted, "Finally!"

The doctor told me to sit and said that he would be back shortly with some clothes. I told him thank you and that I would wait for his return. The world turned slowly as I waited for him to come back. When the doctor finally arrived, he said, "Sorry, but our lost and found is empty." He then handed me a hospital gown and seemed to be laughing as he continued, saying, "But, I found this." I took the gown and replied, "Very funny." He turned to the door and told me, "I'm sorry but it's all we had. You can leave when you're ready.

I unfolded the gown and put it on. I felt like an idiot as I tried to cover my ass (literally) with both hands as I headed out of the room. I opened the door and entered the hallway looking around hoping that no one was spying on me. Down the hall the doctor was about to go see another patient. As he noticed standing in the hallway like a deer caught in the headlights, he called to me and asked me to wait; he had something to tell me. I stood there shaking from the cold breeze and looking side to side to see how many people were pointing fingers and laughing; thankfully no one was.

A few moments later the doctor came within arm's reach and stood nearly toe to toe with me. He extended his hand out in front of him signaling he wanted to shake hands. I thought for a moment then finally reached forward and shook his hand with firm grip. As he released my hand from his own, he said, "You're a great dad." I thanked him for his kind comment, and he continued, "What's their names?" I tugged the gown closed behind me as I felt a draft go up my rear end and the hair stand up on the back of my neck. I then replied, "Sasha and Gabbie." He smiled warmly and replied, "Their lucky to have you." He wasted no time and began to quickly walk away; I assumed he needed to attend to other patients. He was halfway down the hall when I called out to him, saying, "No, doc."

He turned back around to face me completely as he heard he say; I struggled to speak my throat was raw and the pain of vomiting continually had eroded my esophagus from the stomach acids and grotesque bile which spewed from up from my bowels and splashed across the floor like a broken water pipe. I told him, "I'm the lucky one." He then saluted me like an army General would and disappeared behind green curtains at the end of the hall. I lowered my head slightly and whispered softly, "Don't worry, girls." I couched into my hand then continued, "I'm coming."

PSALM 100

Shout for joy to the LORD, all the earth.

Worship the LORD with gladness; come
Before him with joyful songs.

Know that the LORD is God. It is he who made us,
and we are his; we are his people, the
Sheep of his pasture.

Enter his gates with thanksgiving and his courts
with praise; give thanks to him and
praise his name.

For the LORD is good and his love endures
forever; his faithfulness continues
through all generations.

"If there are no dogs in Heaven, then when I die, I want to go where they went."

- Will Rogers

CHAPTER FIFTEEN
DAY OF RUIN

PT. 4
THE STRENGTH OF GOD

The next morning, I stood outside in the cold smoking one cigarette after another. I knew Sasha and Gabbie were upstairs waiting for my return but as long as I was close by, I knew no harm would come to them. I stood in the driveway of the house and rested my arms on the wire fence (which was rusted and old) and began to think about what to do next? I worried that maybe the doctor was right? I even agreed that perhaps I should have stayed in the hospital and gotten the treatment that he so strongly recommended?

I finished smoking my last cigarette and then entered my house and quickly ran up the stairs to my bedroom. It was nearing 4:00pm and all I wanted to do was lay down and rest. However, a few moments later my phone rang, and I answered it quickly; it was my father. I lifted the phone to my ear and greeted him warmly while keeping my eyes shut; I had an intense headache that was worsening by the minute. "Hey, dad," I said. "What's up?" There was a commotion in the background, and I could barely hear him as he replied, "You feeling any better?" I strained to open my eyes; my vision was hazy. I squinted and reached for a cup of water that was next to my bed. I took a sip of water then quickly placed the cup down. "Yea, dad. I'm fine." I lifted myself up the placed one hand on the mattress and braced myself in an upright position. "What did the doctor say?" My father asked curiously. I threw my legs over the edge of the bed and stood up. I pinned the phone between my ear and shoulder the placed both hands on the wall and shimmed over to the light switch.

I slide my hand up and across the wall and in a swift motion flicked on the light switch. I was momentarily blinded as the light consumed the room refracting off the walls and ceiling and strikingly cornea with an intense ray of light. I squinted my eyes and told my father, "The doctor said I'm dehydrated," I cleared my throat then continued, "I just need to drink more water, that's all." The phone nearly slipped from my neck as I sat back down on the bed. "Just rest," my father replied. "Drink a lot of water. It'll help." I shut my eyes and laid my head down on the pillow and replied, "I'm sure you're right, dad." I heard another phone ring; it was then landline. "I gotta run," he said quickly. "Feel better." I then heard him pick up the other receiver. "I'll call you later." I said goodbye and then he hung up the phone.

I didn't bother to press the end button on the phone rather I just let the phone slip from my neck and fall on the bed. I moaned then rubbed my forehead with one hand and said aloud, "This fucking headache just won't go away." I opened my eyes slightly and looked at Sasha then turned my head and smiled at Gabbie. "I'm sorry, girls," I exhaled a long sigh then continued, "I know you want to go out, but I can barely stand." Sasha began to whimper and Gabbie inched closer to me and then laid her head on my chest. "What is it girls?" I said while quickly glancing back and forth to Sasha and Gabbie trying to reassure them not to worry. I then lowered my hand from my forehead and gently pet Gabbie on the top of her head and asked, "What's wrong, Gabs?" Of course, she didn't answer me. In fact, all she did was look up at me with her big, bright brown eyes; yet somehow, we were communicating. This look reminded me of when I heard a friend of my say, "I have never seen a dog look at a human being the way Gabbie looks at you." I smiled down at Gabbie and I could feel tears forming behind my eyes; they were tears of joy. I told her while trying not to cry, "I love you too, Gab, Gab."

Suddenly, Sasha began to whimper louder and louder. I began to get the distinct feeling that she was trying to tell me something (or perhaps warn me). Gabbie then smashed her paw on top of my stomach; the sudden impact made me jerk away. "Easy, Gabs," I said while adjusting my position on the mattress. Sasha then quickly stood up. She turned her head to one side as if she was listening to a high-pitched sound that only she could hear. "Sit, Sash." I told her. "You're gonna fall off the bed." As you can imagine Sasha didn't listen. Instead, she stepped forward and put her entire body weight on my stomach. The muscles in my stomach tightened and I was trying hard to breath. "Sash!" My voice was strained as I shouted at her. "What are you doing?"

After a few minutes of pleading with both Sasha and Gabbie to go to opposite sides of the bed I finally declared that I would have to force them off me. "Damn it, Sash." I shouted while I yanked the blanket hoping it would throw off her balance and make her step back. I shouted at Gabbie, "Gabbers!" I then tried to slide out from underneath the blanket and to the edge of the bed. "What is wrong with you two?" I threw the blanket down onto the bed and then stood up completely. Sasha cringed like she always did when she knew she was about to get an ass whooping. I gritted my teeth and smacked Sasha on her rear end. "Now, is not the time for this shit, Sash!" I yelled at her. I then pointed at Gabbie and told her sternly, "I'm mad at you too, Gabs."

I sat on the bed and calmly called to Sasha to come to my side. At first, she wouldn't come so I grabbed her gently by her collar and pulled her close to me. I hugged her and apologized for smacking her. Gabbie raised her head off the bed and started wagging her tail wildly from side to side. After a few brief moments she rolled over onto her back and waited for me to pet her belly. I laughed then kissed Sasha on the top of her head. I lightly patted Gabbie on her belly and hugged Sasha at my side while saying, "I know life sucks right now, girls. But it doesn't matter because we have each other. Sooner or later everything will work out. I promise." I continued petting Gabbie on her stomach while simultaneously petting Sasha on her head.

After a few minutes of cuddling with both of them I gently shoved Gabbie over the edge of the bed next to the wall. As I did Sasha jumped down off the bed and again started to whimper. "Ugh! Sash! Come on!" I pleaded with her repeatedly to be quiet. "What's wrong, girl? I leaned forward off the bed and asked her while occasionally mumbling incoherent baby babble, "You gotta go pee? Is that is?" I figured that I would never hear the end of Sasha's whining if I didn't at least attempt to take her out. However, as I stood up Sasha would go into a barking frenzy; as much I yelled at her to stop, she wouldn't. "Fuck, Sash!" I was becoming angrier with each passing second. "Shut the..." Just then Gabbie stood completely up on the bed; she wobbled from side to side but quickly re-gained her balance. She stared at me intently and glanced back and forth to Sasha and then to Gabbie; I couldn't make heads or tails of what all the commotion was about?

Sasha's barking became more ferocious by the minute; thankfully my roommate wasn't home to hear all the noise. I stood there dumbfounded at Sasha's rambunctious behavior; it reminded me of when she was a puppy. After a few minutes Gabbie too barked loudly (but, only once). I looked at her then took a step back to the bed to comfort her. Instantly, I grabbed my head with both hands. An immense pain surged through my skull. I clenched my eyes tightly shut and the muscles in my jaw tightened. I hobbled over to the bed and fell forward nearly missing the bed completely. I was half on and half off the mattress with my feet planted firmly on the floor to keep me from sliding downward. Sasha dashed forward and jumped back up onto the bed and began to sniff my face. I moved my head in all directions; her wet nose was tickling my cheek.

After a few minutes the pain subsided, and I opened my eyes and began to breath heavily. "Shit," I muttered softly. "This is bad." My body quaked and I nearly hit the ceiling as Sasha barked directly into my ear. I turned abruptly and stared into her face; I saw worry in her eyes. I smiled out of the corner of my mouth and said, "Don't worry, Sash. I'm okay." However, only minutes later I would come to realize just how dire the situation really was. I attempted to stand up but as I did the room began to spin violently in circles. Seconds later I lost complete control over the muscles in my legs. I clenched my eyes tightly shut as I fell face first and slammed onto the ground. Sasha began to whine and Gabbie rushed to the edge of the bed. I couldn't speak and was barely able to breath. I patted my pants pocket only to realize that my phone was still on the bed.

Slowly I pushed myself up off the floor and up onto my hands and knees; the pain was unbearable. As I moved to the bed to try and recover my phone the pain intensified. Finally, fell back down onto the floor. I lied there breathing heavily and staring at Sasha and Gabbie. I couldn't stop wondering what would happen to them if I couldn't recover? Or even if I was to die? Yet, somehow, I was able to roll over onto my back where my condition to become slightly better. However, the ceiling light was directly overhead which forced me to raise one arm and hide my face.

While lying on the floor images flashed in my mind of all the times, I found myself arguing with former girlfriends; listening to them as they told me I was irresponsible and unable able to care for two dogs. Suddenly, I felt as if they were right and it infuriated me. I gathered my breath and roared like a wild beast. After a few seconds I began to sweat profusely, and the room began to spin. Then, like all the times prior my vision went black and moments later I was unconscious.

PSALM 6

*LORD, do not rebuke me in your anger or
discipline me in your wrath.*

*Have mercy on me, LORD, for I am faint; heal me,
LORD, for my bones are in agony.*

*My soul is in deep anguish. How long,
LORD, how long?*

*Turn, LORD, and deliver me; save me because of
your unfailing love.*

*Among the dead no one proclaims your name.
Who praises you from the grave?*

*I am worn out from my groaning. All night long
I flood my bed with weeping and drench
my couch with tears.*

*My eyes grow weak with sorrow; they fail
because of all my foes.*

*Away from me, all you who do evil, for the LORD
has heard my weeping.*

*The LORD has heard my cry for mercy;
the LORD accepts my prayer.*

"My fashion philosophy is, if you're not covered in dog hair, your life is empty."

– Elayne Boosler

CHAPTER SIXTEEN
DAY OF RUIN

PT. 5
THE ARMOR OF GOD

After reading the above chapter(s) some readers may say, "That can't be true, Drew? Can it?" Well, medical records and my father's testimony would surely beg to differ. Still, upon hearing you ask this I would of course be confused by your statement (should you be thinking such a thing?) Undoubtedly, I would reply, "If you make will it the strength of the human will is unbreakable." Yet, knowing that you're an inquisitive reader you will continue, saying, "But, why wouldn't you just call an ambulance and get treated? Why ostracize all the people who tried to help you?" Sadly, I cannot give you a simple answer to your question. Instead, let me reiterate to you what was told to me by a very smart woman who gave me sound advice not too long ago. She said, "To love someone is to die a little bit more for him or her each day." Those words are truer today than they were on the very day they were said to me. I guess you could say that is why I refused treatment; the reason why I was ready to die. Maybe it makes more sense if I simply admit that I love them far more then I love myself - Sasha and Gabbie, that is.

Let me now bring you back to the night when I stared into the abyss and watched my life disintegrate to ash. However, like the Phoenix who rises from the ash I too was about to have a radical rebirth of sorts. Yet, to accomplish what many people have dubbed "unbelievable" I would have to first go deeper into Hell then I had ever gone before. Soon, I would find out just how strong I really was...

I awoke to hear my phone vibrating on the bed. I ignored it, however I was in no mood to talk to anyone. A few moments passed until I heard the screen door outside the house creak open. I then heard a faint fumbling noise outside on the porch and then suddenly the deadbolt snapped open; the reinforced hardwood door gently swung open and the hinges squeaked. I lifted my head slightly off the floor and stared up through the blinds of the only window in the room; I saw grey clouds looming in the sky; something told me it was going to snow. I then sat upright as I heard someone knock on my door. Strangely, the sickness I had been suffering from for nearly two weeks was gone. What could have cured the illness that I was fighting so desperately to resist? I had no answers only more questions. However, even though I was feeling much better I still had a few random moments of vertigo and occasional headaches.

I heard footsteps come up the stairs and then moments later there was knock on my door. I got up off the floor and unlocked the bedroom door and upon opening it I saw my landlord glaring at me. Before I could speak, she said, "Drew, we're asking you and the roommate to be out by the end of the month; my sister and her kids are going to move in." Surprisingly, however, I was upset, angry or, even, shocked. A few seconds passed until Sasha barked loudly and my landlord jumped back in fright. My landlord then spoke; her voice was shaky as she said, "Your Pitfall is very mean." I looked slightly over my shoulder at Sasha and then turned back to my landlord and replied, "No, she doesn't like you." I then began to shut the door, but something made me swing it open and say, "And she's not a Pitfall. She's a Boxer, you dumb bitch!" I then slammed the door shut and listened as she walked down the stairs and out the front door.

I put my back against the door and Sasha came over to me and I leaned forward and pet her on her head. She cringed at first. Maybe she thought I was made at her? I then kneeled down and said, "Good girl, Sash. Fuck that bitch! We don't this place. It's a dump anyway." I then began to pack my stuff and moments later my phone had rung again. This time I picked it up and on heart a faint, raspy voice on the end of the phone ask, "Is this Drew?" I wiped my forehead with the palm of my hand and replied, "Yea, this is Drew. How can I help you?" What happened next would be shocking to say the least. I listened as the woman asked, "I'm renting a room and I wanted to reach out and ask if you were still looking?" At first, I was awestruck and was at a loss of words. "Is this a joke?" I thought. It seemed to coincidental but then again it didn't. I happily replied, "Actually, yes, I am still looking." I told her.

That afternoon I boarded the subway and went to see the room which was located in Richmond Hill. It took only fifteen minutes until said, "Okay. I'll take it!" The next morning, I called a van which specialized in moving pets. I waited for about a half hour for the van to arrive. When it did, I moved all my stuff to the driveway. I placed my belongings in the van then went upstairs and brought Sasha down and then went back up to the bedroom and got Gabbie and put them both in the back seat of the van. I told the driver, "Let's get the Hell outta!" He then hit the gas pedal and we sped out of the driveway and not the main road. It took about twenty minutes to get to my new apartment.

When we arrived, I brought Sasha and Gabbie upstairs and threw my garage bags full of clothes down onto the floor. However, I had to go back to my previous apartment to get my television and computer. I asked my landlord if he could kindly watch Sasha and Gabbie. Instead he offered to drive me back to my old apartment with Sasha and Gabbie. I was happy and thanked him for his kindness. I told the driver of the van I wouldn't need him to drive me back and gave him a twenty-dollar tip.

Sasha and Gabbie hadn't had much time to settle in when I said, "Sorry, girls. We got go back. Promise it won't take long." It didn't take king for all three of us to get in the car and head back to my old apartment. I remember feeling enraged as we were heading back Flushing; I didn't know what I would do, if anything if the landlord was there to get the keys. Yet, in a strange way I was hoping she would be.

We arrived and I quickly ran up the driveway and opened the front door. I hurdled the stairs and went to my old bedroom. To my surprise, however, the landlord was in the room and inspecting it for damage. I looked at her with disgust in my eyes. I took the keys out of my pocket and said, "Here." She grabbed them from my hand without hesitation. I walked to the opposite side of the room and picked my television and then began to make my way out of the house. As I exited the bedroom, I heard her say, "It's nothing personal, Drew. But family is family." I placed the television down on the floor in front of me and replied, "You can't even imagine what I have been through over the last few weeks." She twirled her thumbs and seemed distracted by her phone; I could hear it vibrating in her pocket. She took the phone from her pocket while saying, "I wish you the best, Drew." I was insulted as Hell after hearing her talk to me with such disrespect. I looked her up and down and felt the sudden urge to spit on her. I even imagined snatching the phone from her hands and smashing to pieces on the ground. I shouted at her, "Hey!" She lifted her head and calmly replied, "My sister will be here..." I interrupted her and told her angrily, "Fuck you and fuck your sister!" Her eyes bulged. She was horrified.

I could feel my muscles tighten; the tendons in my arms and legs were about to snap. I told her, "Pray you never see me again." She replied and said with a look of confusion strewn across her face. "Did I do something to upset you, Drew?" I couldn't believe what I was hearing. I had to leave quickly; I couldn't hold back my anger anymore. "You have some fucking nerve!" I told her. She then looked to her phone; she had a new text message. I then stepped forward and tried to pin her against the wall. "Every time you open your mouth I want to vomit," I said with look of disgust. "I know why you want me out..." I pointed out into the hallway. "She told me." She then crunched her face and replied, "Who told you? Their lying!" Her voice was filled with a tone of confusion. "The fucking roommate, dumb ass!" I shook my head and clenched my fists and continued. "Don't fuck with me!" Her face had a genuine look of, "I don't know what you're talking about?" But I knew better. Like the old saying goes, "You can't bullshit a bullshit artist."

I stared into her face and angrily said, "It's my dogs, right?" She then attempted to leave the room. As she walked past me, I said, "Yea, I thought so." She held her phone out in front of her and looked back at me and said, "My father is afraid." I then scoffed and replied, "Afraid of me? Or of them? She sighed and replied, "Of the dogs." I then smirked. My voice was threatening as I replied, "Good. He should be." She then continued to make her way out of the room. I called to her as she walked down the stairs, "You're a piece of shit! you hear me?" She then called to me from downstairs, "You need to leave, Drew. Now!" I grabbed the television and hurried out the room and down the stairs. I nearly knocked her over as I pushed opened the door with my shoulder and headed to the van. I forgot that I had left the van door was open and as I got closer to the van Sasha got excited and began barking as she my former landlord walk up behind me.

I turned around and found myself nose to nose with her. She told me in a clam, soothing voice, "Like I said - It's nothing personal, Drew. Really." I spit at her feet and then replied, "It is to me." She put her phone into her purse and replied, "I'm sorry you feel that way." I snorted insinuating that I was going to spit at her again; this time I wanted to spit in her face. But, I didn't. I then responded to her lame remarks by saying, "If you don't like them, then you don't like me. That makes it personal." She said nothing and just walked back to her car which was parked on the street. I watched her as she opened the driver's door and started the ignition. I flicked up my middle finger as she looked at me through the passenger's side window. She then sped away without a word.

To her surprise a few days later her father (the one who didn't like Sasha) was served a lawsuit from small claims court. After receiving she called me and told me that it was unnecessary to file a lawsuit against her father. I listened to her plead for me to drop the suit as she claimed that it would tarnish her record as a landlord. I remember asking her, "Landlord? I thought your sister was moving in?" I guess he figured I wouldn't remember when she said that. I refused to drop the suit and said something to her along the lines of, "Other than my family there are only two things in this world that you can't fuck with - Sasha and Gabbie."

For nearly six months I kept her in limbo while constantly reminding her that I had every intention of a full-blown legal battle over her head. Finally, in September of 2015 I dropped the suit after receiving compensation in the form my security deposit (this money kept me alive and helped me relocate only three months later). I will never forget the last text I sent her when I said, "There are better ways get what you want. Hurting me or my daughters was the least favorable thing you could have ever done. Now, I proved my point. See you in the next life!" All she could reply back with was, "Daughters? You have two daughters?" After reading her text, I muttered to myself, "What a stupid asshole."

She was right about thing, though. The lawsuit did tarnish her reputation as a landlord. Only a few days later I filed the lawsuit. as the months passed, I came to find out that she that she had no other recourse but put the house up for sale. It seemed that other potential renters were not favor of a landlord who had recently been sued by a former tenant. Truthfully, I had no remorse for her whatsoever. Yet, I often do regret not spitting in her face but in the end, I got what was rightfully mine. So, in the end I felt vindicated even if I still resented her for her action against Sasha, Gabbie and I.

Since facing those horrible days when I found myself teetering on the brink of death, I have told many people that I had wished I had perished from strange sickness that consumed me. It is an undeniable fact of life that the pain I experienced over those two grueling weeks was great. Yet, it was nothing in comparison to what was about to transpire next. Only weeks later my life would lose all purpose, and I would find myself staring into the bottom of a bottle and drinking myself into a state of stupidity. Though, as unbelievable as it may sound that was when I found Him - God. It was at that exact moment that God had finally made His presence known. After all these years He would deny me no more. However, what was He saying? Would I be able to figure out what, if anything He wanted me to hear before it was too late? Only time would tell...

"To sit with a dog on a hillside on a glorious afternoon is to be back in Eden, where doing nothing was not boring; it was peace."

- Milan Kundera

CHAPTER SEVENTEEN
AFTER YOU BUT BEFORE ME

I remember it vividly. I had just returned home from a hard day's work in Manhattan; I had spent nearly seven hours doing live video editing for a reality television show. Before heading upstairs, I stopped to get the mail which my landlord left at the bottom of the stairs. I glanced at what I assumed was a card which had the return address of the veterinarian's office in the top left-hand corner. At first, I didn't think anything of it. I figured it was nothing more than a card like those I receive each year from my dentist who wishes me a happy birthday (even though I can't ever remember his).

I walked inside and closed the front door behind me. As I headed upstairs, I began to open the card. I wasn't able to read and walk at the same time, so I stopped about halfway up the stairwell. I began to re-

read the card (this time paying attention to what it said) and felt a warm sensation come over me; it was a condolence card from the vet. I said aloud, "How sweet." But, within seconds I would become dizzy and faint, fall down the stairs and wake up in a state of disarray.

As I looked over the card, I came to notice that there was an imprint of Sasha's paws in the empty white space at the top of the card. Upon seeing her paw prints I was consumed by a feeling I never experienced before; one I can't even describe no matter how hard I try. Immediately I broke down into tears and cried out, "Oh, God!" My knees buckled and I grasped tightly onto the railing beside me with one hand. Though, it was no use. Within seconds everything went black and I rolled down the stairs; crashing into boxes and debris scattered sporadically on the bottom landing. I don't know how long I laid there (probably no more than a few seconds). When I awoke, I found the card intact and lying face down and still on my chest. I grabbed it gently and held it up in front of me. I sat up and looked into the card and caressed the imprint with my fingertips. All I could mutter was, "It should have been me."

Over the course of the next few weeks things became increasingly harder to manage. I remember thinking that I hadn't taken enough pictures of Sasha; I wanted to litter the walls and ceiling with her image. Over the years I was irresponsible and allowed the pictures to get lost. I had so many great one (even a few of Sasha and Gabbie swimming in my parent's pool).

I inadvertently allowed the sadness to get the better of me and trick me into believing that I was a bad "parent." People told me over and over again, "Drew, you gave her an amazing life!" Upon hearing these words, I was often times overcome by thoughts which ran widely through my mind such as: how amazing was it when we were homeless? How amazing was it when I was reduced to eating out of garbage cans, and recycling bottles for a messily five cents, and, even, sleeping at a hotel while never knowing what would happen next?

No matter how many times I told myself, "She was happy" there always seemed to be some random thought from the past of a time when I overreacted because of her behavior that made me doubt everything I believed. Over time these thoughts which entered my mind for seemingly no reason began to eat away at my very soul. It wasn't until my father said to me, "Give Gabbie a hug; hold her and tell her you love her. I'm sure she misses Sasha too" that I began to find the strength I thought I had lost forever.

That afternoon I left house but not before do as my father instructed and kissed Gabbie on her head and told her I loved her. I noticed that the clouds were turning grey and I was certain it was going to rain at any moment. Though, I didn't care. I hurried and picked up my backpack and carefully placed the card in the front pocket. I walked down the stairs and opened the front door and felt a cold breeze hit my face. I stepped off the stairs and out into the driveway then lowered my sunglasses and looked up into the ominous clouds which seemed to be taunting me. I recall seeing my landlord off to one side and hearing him ask me, "Drew, you going somewhere? You need a lift?" I told him thanks but said I'd rather walk and assured him I would be back soon. He asked me where I was going and I replied, "To the framer. I want to get this card I got framed." He nodded then replied, "Okay. Be careful. I'll see you soon."

The framer was two and half miles away and the odds of getting before it started raining seemed impossible. I thought that maybe I should have accepted a ride from my landlord? However, this was something I needed to do alone. Though, I worried that if it did begin to rain the card could possibly get wet and the ink would run, and the card would be ruined. I knew there was no time to waste.

Thankfully, the majority of the walk was dry; not one drop fell froth sky. However, as I got within a block of the framer the skies opened up and the rain hit the ground like bullets falling from the sky. I dashed underneath an awning and shimmed along the edge of the building. A few minutes later I got the framer and quickly pushed the door open and entered.

An elderly Korean woman greeted me and asked me if I was dropping off or picking up. I took my backpack from off my back and gently pulled the card out from the front pocket. I laid the card on the glass countertop and opened it and told her I wanted it framed. She asked me what kind of framing I preferred, and I told her that I had sixty dollars to my name but didn't want something that would fall apart in a month.

She walked in a small room adjacent to the counter and took out a frame that was silver and red. I pointed at the frame and said, "That's perfect!" She told the cost and I agreed and then she took the card and carefully placed it in a manila envelope. She asked me my name and wrote it on the folder. She told me it would be ready to be picked up in a week or less. I smiled and told her thank you and then left.

As I stepped out into the street, I was immediately soaked by the pouring rain. In a strange way I was glad it was raining, however; the droplets of water running down my face would surely camouflage my tears. I must have cried the entire walk home. I remember saying, "I love you, Sash" over and over again. Then, without trying I remembered the words my father had told me; I could hear them echo in my mind, "Give Gabbie a hug and tell her you love her." It was then that I took a pack of cigarettes from my pant pocket and held back the flood of tears which wanted to erupt from my eyes. I light the cigarette and said, "I won't let you down, Sash. I will keep my promise even if it kills me." Suddenly, I was overcome with great strength that empowered my mind.

About forty-five minutes later I arrived back at my house. I unlocked the door; I was happy no one was home. I went up to my bedroom and opened the door and saw Gabbie sleep peacefully on the couch. I dropped my bag on the floor and rushed to the edge of the couch and kneeled down and pet Gabbie on her head. She woke up and was surprised to see me staring at her from only a few inches away. I smiled at her and said, "I miss, Sash, Gab, Gab, but no matter what I won't let her down." I kissed her on the tip of her nose then continued, "Or you. I will find a way."

A tear fell from my eye and I got up and walked to my computer. I sat down in the chair then turned back and looked at Gabbie who was now fully awake. I spun around in the chair and asked her rhetorically, "What do you say we get the Hell out of New York? Huh, Gabs." She stared at me as if she was about to answer my question, but I knew she couldn't. I sniffled and held back more tears then continued, saying, "Maybe some place far, far away?"

Gabbie slid down the couch and landed softly on the floor. She took a few steps to her water bowl then laid down and drank lazily. After she was done, she went to my bed and jumped up and put her paw on my bed (it was hard for her to jump on the mattress now that she was almost twelve years old). Though, even though she couldn't jump like she used when she was younger, she was still pretty agile for a dog her age.

I got up from the chair and said, "Okay, girl. One second..." I grabbed her gently under her belly and lifted her up onto the bed. She laid down on my pillow but kept one eye open in order to keep a watchful eye on me; I knew she could feel my emotions and that she was worried about me. I returned to the computer but felt compelled to turn back a few moments later and look at Gabbie. Instantly, I could feel my heart breaking as I realized that Sasha was no longer there to keep her company; that Gabbie had lost her sister.

I stopped what I was doing and went over to the bed and laid down next to Gabbie; I couldn't let her be alone. I stretched and a moment later she laid her head on my stomach and shut her eyes. I pet her softly on the top of her head and told her, "It's me, you and Sash forever." Gabbie grunted like she always did when she just wants to die to shut up and let her fall asleep. A few seconds passed and I sprung up from the mattress and shuffled to the foot the bed. Gabbie was startled and seemed confused by my actions. I turned back to her and with excitement in my voice said, "We're leaving, Gabs." I got up off the bed and dialed my friend who lived only a few miles away.

The phone rang three times and finally he picked it up. I said hello and he asked me how I was doing? I told him I was leaving New York and needed to save all my money to prepare for the unseen forces that may try and stop me. As I began to tell him my plan he said, "Drew, shut up!" I was shocked. He continued, "You don't even have to ask..." I interrupted him and questioned, "Ask what?" He laughed the replied, "You need a place to stay?" I was surprised. Did he read mind? I thought. "Yea," I replied. "But I'm not leaving, Gabbie." He said without hesitation, "Bring her! Don't worry about it." That evening I tore up the rent check I was going to turn into my landlord then informed that I would be leaving the following day. To say that he was pissed would be an understatement. Still, who was he to tell me what to do?

It turned out that leaving that place was one of the best things I could have ever done. However, the next four months would be trying to say the least. Yet, as the holiday season approached it seemed that fate was about to come full circle. And while my grief worsened by the day, I would soon become be privy to a revelation which make all the pain, all suffering, and all the heartache worthwhile.

I don't know how it all happened. I will never understand the will of God, or why he put me on this earth in the first place. Still, what I do know is that Sasha and Gabbie kept me alive when I should have been dead. It was in knowing this which allowed me to turn my tragedy into triumph and escape the nightmare which has followed me like a black cloud for over a decade.

I told myself that it was up to me to change my fate. You see, I could either have given up and gone nowhere fast. Or, I could choose to allow the forces of the universe to guide me to a destination that seemed too good to be true. And as hard as it was for me to find peace and happiness, I told myself that I had to succeed but not for me, but for Gabbie. The following four months would test my resolve and tax my strength beyond belief. Yet, by the time it was over Gabbie and I would finally be free.

PSALM 129

*"They have greatly oppressed me from my
youth," let Israel say; "They have greatly
oppressed me from my youth, but they
have not gained the victory
over me.*

*Plowmen have plowed my back and made
their furrows long. But the LORD is righteous; he has
cut me free from the cords of the wicked."*

*May all who hate Zion be turned back in shame.
May they be like grass on the roof, which
withers before it can grow; a reaper
cannot fill his hands with it, nor one
who gathers fill his arms.*

*May those who pass by not say to them, "The
blessing of the LORD be on you; we bless
you in the name of the LORD."*

"I wonder what goes through his mind when he sees us peeing in his water bowl."

- Penny Ward Moser

CHAPTER EIGHTEEN
ASHES TO ASHES

It was undoubtedly the hardest day of my life and one I will never forget. For two weeks I counted the days while waiting for a phone call from the vet. Up until now I had tricked my brain into believing that I would get a call (from the vet) who would tell me to come and pick up Sasha; that she was healthy and eager to go home. Sadly, the call that eventually came would not be a homecoming. In fact, it would devastate me in ways to complicated to explain.

I woke that morning sometime around nine o'clock. Something told me to keep my phone close by. Less than a half hour later my phone rang. The area code began with 718 and somehow, I knew that it was the vet calling me. It took about four rings before I picked it up and said, asking rhetorically, "Hello?" Before answering the phone, I took a deep breath and buried all my emotions deep inside me. Finally, I answered the phone and heard a lady on the other end ask, "Mr. Glick?" I replied quickly, "Yes." She then continued and said, "This is the animal hospital. We have Sasha's ashes. You can pick up the urn anytime today." I pretended as if nothing was out of the ordinary as I replied, "Okay. I'll be there shortly.

The vet was roughly a twenty-minute walk from my house. As I grabbed my jacket and headed outside, I felt a cool breeze gently hit my face. I patted my pants pockets and realized I had left my cigarettes upstairs. I rushed back inside and headed up the stairs then unlocked my apartment door and snatched the box of cigarettes off of my desk. I kissed Gabbie on the top of her head (she was sleeping on the couch) then ran down the stairs; I nearly fell face first onto the ground as I reached the last step. I opened the front door with such force that it slammed against the wall behind it rattling the hinges (I'm not sure if I was angry or scared?) I walked down the driveway and closed the gate behind me then took a deep breath and light a cigarette; I smoked it slowly as I walked out of the neighborhood.

I walked down the side street then speed up my pace as I got to the main road. I kept thinking about holding back my emotions; I feared that once I grasped the urn in my arms, I would cry uncontrollably. I refused to allow the vet to see me in such a state of despair.

Yet, the closer I got the vet the harder it was for me to keep my composure. I lowered my sunglasses as I started to have memories of my last day with Sasha when I held her on my lap and told her I loved her. I began to sniffle then moments later tears fell down my face. I muttered aloud, "I miss you, Sash."

Suddenly, a subway car roared loudly overhead; the ground below my feet shook violently. I looked up and saw the train as it sped down the tracks towards Manhattan. I glanced off into the distance and saw the yellow brick of the veterinary building; I was almost there. I took a few steps and then I stopped dead in my tracks and turned around began to walk in the opposite direction. "I can't do this..." I whispered softly to myself.

I stood there frozen and unable to move. I had suddenly lost my ability to even the simplest of motor functions, such as walking, or even speaking. I couldn't fathom the idea of picking up Sasha's urn. I didn't want to accept that was gone and all I had to remember her by was an urn. I then started to wail and scream at the top of my lungs. The people around me scattered like Ants running from a fire. My chest inflated like a balloon and I began to growl and moan. Next to me was a steel girder that held up the subway tracks overhead. I glanced to my side and that was when everything turned red. I lunged forward and slammed my fist into the steel girder. Immediately my hand began to throb; I was certain I broke my hand. A moment later I began to cry and then my knees buckled, and I fell forward and collapsed up against the girder. I sat there crying while occasionally wiping the tears from my face. I watched as people walked past me and glanced down at me from the corner of their eye. I spit at one gentleman who passed me by as if I was a piece of garbage. He snarled at me and then continued to walk down the sidewalk.

Even though I was being tormented by outlandish thoughts of paranoia I was growing increasingly angry that not one person out of a possible dozen or more even stopped to offer me help. This fact disgusted me. After a moment or two I pushed myself up off the ground and regained my composure. As I stood there trying to find the strength to continue to the vet's office I snarled at few people and even shouted at a young girl, "Fuck you too then!" I then tugged on my shirt and wiped my face one last time.

I started walking to the building and all the while thinking about how I would react once I her the urn in my hands? I worried if I would lash out like I did only moment prior? Would I strike the nurse? Or would I go into an unstoppable frenzy and take my angry out on innocent people? I was only a few minutes from arriving at the vet's office when my cell phone rang. It was my father. I remember looking down at the screen and asking myself, "How do you do it, dad?" I answered the phone and said hello and he asked me if I was okay? I told him that I was on my way to the vet to pick up the urn, about what had just happened, and that I didn't feel safe picking up the urn by myself. I wiped tears from my eyes as I admitted to that him that I felt like I was a danger to people around me, and, even, myself.

I can't recall what my father and I spoke about. But, if not for that phone call I think the outcome of that afternoon would have been far different then it was. My father always had a way of speaking to me that helped me find peace of mind. When I finally arrived at the front door to the vet's office I listened as my father told me, "Just remember - this doesn't mean that you have to stop loving, Sasha."

As I heard him say those words my knees buckled, and I shut my eyes and nearly fainted. He then continued, saying, "I know you and I know how much this hurts. I also know that you are stronger than anyone I know." I then opened my eyes and took a few steps towards the front door. My voice cracked as I replied, "Thanks, dad." I placed my hand on the doorknob and was about to open the door when he interjected and said, "Son," he paused; I gathered that he was trying to console me? He then continued, "Remember how you feel today." I was confused and furrowed my brow and replied, "This is one day, dad I hope to forget." His voice grew loud; he was agitated, angry almost. "No! Don't." He shouted into the phone. He then continued, "This is the day you will remember when you ask yourself, "How did all this happen?"" I was even more confused then before. I knew he wasn't trying to upset me further, but I had no idea why he would tell me to hold onto such horrible emotions and memories that I can't bear to think of?

Before entering the waiting area of the vet's office, I asked him over and over again to tell me what he was talking about? Yet, he refused to tell me. All he said was, "The day you stand on the mountain and look down upon the world you will know what I mean." It took me nearly two years to understand the importance of our conversation that day. Only now do I fully comprehend what he said to me and why he said it in the first place.

Not too long after this conversation occurred, I called my father and said, "I stood on the mountain, dad." At first, he said nothing. Though, I got the sense he was happy and, even, smiling. After a few moments he replied, "Good. Now, go climb your way to the top." Prior to me calling my father with excitement in my voice to tell him I discovered the secret behind his riddle I was looking for hope but sadly found none. In fact, the day that I found myself attacking steel girders, spitting and shouting profanity at random strangers was a day that I lost all hope that I had any further purpose on the planet earth; I asked myself what was keeping me from committing suicide. It was an obvious answer of course but one I was too blind to see while in such a state of disarray. You see I had lost faith humanity; in their ability to show empathy and compassion for a person enduring inconceivable heartache. I was embarrassed and humiliated in a way to consider myself a part of such a cruel and hurtful species. But, what choice did I have?

As we come to the end of this chapter, I am certain that there are readers who would like to know what occurred after I entered the vet's office and found the courage to hold the Sasha's urn in my bare hands? Sadly, I would prefer not to write about those moments as they are very personal to both me and Sasha alike. However, what I can tell you is that soon after this terrible day a beacon of hope would arrive which illuminated the darkness from over three thousand miles away. This beacon would once and for all reveal a path to a place I have come to call, "Eden"; a place that would revitalize my soul and change my life forever.

Yet, reaching this beacon would require more courage, more strength and more faith then I could ever have thought possible by single human being. Soon, God would descend from the Heavens and ask me a straightforward simple, yet profound question, "How bad do want it?" My answer would shock even myself.

\

"The more one gets to know of men, the more one values dogs."

- Alphonse Toussenel

CHAPTER NINETEEN
WHISPERS FROM HEAVEN

It was May 13th, 2015. The day was warm, yet a cool breeze swirled around me which kept the burning heat from scorching my skin. I was taking Gabbie to the to get a check-up at the vet. We had been walking for about twenty minutes when Gabbie and I stopped to enjoy the nice weather; Gabbie sniffed the flowers while I sat on a railroad tie and enjoyed a cigarette. About a block away from the animal hospital a young couple (around the age of twenty-five) stopped me and asked if they could pet Gabbie. Oddly they had no idea that she only had three legs (you'd be surprised by the number of people who fail to realize this fact when first encountering Gabbie).

After the couple discovered that she (Gabbie) had only three legs the man seemed to get excited and took out his cell phone and asked if he could take a picture of her? I could tell he adored Gabbie and even his girlfriend (who I assumed was his girlfriend, but I wasn't sure) smiled and said, "She's beautiful." I replied, "Thank you for your kindness" and then nodded to the man and said, "Take as many pictures as you want. She's very photogenic." I called down to Gabbie and said excitedly, "Hey, Gabbie girl!" I wiped a bead of sweat from my brow with one hand and continued, "You want your picture taken, Boo Boo?" I asked her rhetorically. She sat up quickly and smiled then remained still for a few seconds. The man held his phone out in front of him and took a few pictures. I stood in place with Gabbie at my side and held the leash and tried to keep her from looking away. When he was done taking the picture, he asked me simple, yet random questions including where I was from and how long I had Gabbie, and even what happened that caused her to have three legs.

As I was in the mists of a detailed explanation as an older gentleman walking with his daughter (who was no more than thirteen) politely interrupted me and said, "God bless you..." His eyes swelled with happy tears and he then continued, "God bless you for what you are doing for her." I smiled to him then graciously responded, "Thank you, Sir. That means a lot." He replied, "People like you are one in a million." I pet Gabbie on the top of her head then replied, "If I could only find the words to tell you just how truly blessed, I feel..." I paused when a random memory of Sasha flashed in my mind; I smiled (it was the first time I thought of her without crying). I then continued and told him, "They are my angels." I was thankful, however that neither the little girl or her father caught me when I said, "They" rather than "She." I was relived because I was concerned that if asked, I would begin to cry as I told them about Sasha. Then the young girl (whose name I can't recall) called out to me and asked, "What's her name?" I replied happily, "Gabbie. But you can call her Gabbers." The young girl blushed then giggled as she reached forward and gently pet Gabbie on the top of her head. She then said, "Hi Gabbers." A few seconds later she took her father's hand and continued, saying, "I like your name. It's pretty."

Following the casual encounter with the young and her father Gabbie and I sat on a small hill covered with lush grass and dandelions. I remember sitting there picking the dandelions while Gabbie ate them. A few moments later the breeze became stronger and kicked up on dust and debris which I chocked on momentarily. I reached into my front jean pocket and took out a pack of cigarettes and then placed a cigarette in my mouth and raised the lighter readying to strike it. Though, something stopped me dead in my tracks. I lowered the lighter, but the cigarette was still dangling out of my mouth. I looked up into the sky and peered through the fluffy white cloud and into endless sea of blue nothingness.

I sat there and wondered what compelled me to look up into the sky? Almost instantly I snapped my head to one side and the cigarette flew out of her mouth and onto the grass. "What was that?" I thought. I could have sworn someone had put their hand on my shoulder. But, no one was there. Was I imagining things? I picked the cigarette up off the ground and spoke to Gabbie and said, "I'm cracking up, Gab, Gab." I scoffed then placed the cigarette back in my mouth and again raised the lighter and was about to strike it when on the other side of the street I saw a lady walking a Boxer. I was awe struck.

I stared at the lady who's name I didn't know when surprisingly she waved to me from across the street. Without hesitation I waved back. I then called out to her and asked, "What your Boxers name?" Though, a passing bus muffled my voice and she thought I had asked, "What's your name?" She continued walking and put her nose up in the air and her headphones on her ears; she seemed insulted, but I was only trying to be friendly. I thought that maybe I inadvertently gave her the impression that I was trying to pitch her some kind of one liner with the hopes of asking her on a date? I shouted over the road noise and told her, "Your boxer is beautiful." A second or two passed when I watched her change direction and begin to walk towards me. I bite my lip and told Gabbie while faking a smile and staying focused on the lady who I enticed to my location, "Get ready to run, Gabs. I think she wants to kick my ass!"

I remained calm and collected and continued to pick Dandelions while all the while keeping a watchful eye on the woman's demeanor while trying to determine whether or not she was about to pull out mace and spray me with it? As she got close to me, she smiled at me then looked down to Gabbie and said, "Hi beautiful. What's your name?" She then turned back to face me. "I'm sorry but I couldn't hear you over all the noise," she told me while removing her headphones. I waved my hand and acted nonchalant and replied, "It's no problem. I was just asking you what your Boxers name is?" She smiled happily then held the leash tight and told me, "This is Lucy." I nodded to Lucy then said, "Lucy, huh?" I held one arm out to my side and smiled while saying, "Lucy meet Gabbie." Suddenly, Lucy went batshit and was overcome with excitement. I stood up because I was afraid, she would trample me. I tried to hide my face; memories of Sasha flooded my mind and I could feel my eyes ready to burst at any moment and erupt with a waterfall of tears.

Unfortunately, a few moments later however, the woman took notice of my demeanor and asked me, "Are you okay?" I told her politely, "I'm fine. It's just that Lucy reminds me so much of my, Sasha..." I sniffled then continued, "She passed away not too long ago." The woman held one hand over her chest sighed then replied, "I'm so sorry." Without warning she leaned forward and hugged me. I froze in place and was unsure of how to react. I was now getting the feeling that she was coming on to me. It then became obvious that Lucy felt left out, so she decided to jump on me and push me backwards; she wanted the attention just like Sasha always did. I laughed and wiped a tear from my eye and said, "Okay, we see you too, Lucy."

I stood there face to face with a woman who I had never seen before and had only known for a mere fifteen minutes. We spoke about random things and then I found myself talking about Sasha, and, even, Gabbie, for that matter. I then felt a wave of peace fall over me and the world seemed calm and the noise dissipated.

At the end of the conversation I listened as she told me, "Drew, try not to remember the bad things. I know it's hard now, but things will get easier with time. "She smiled and we said our goodbyes and I watched her lead Lucy across the street, and I called out her and replied, "I'll see you around, I guess." She turned slightly and looked over her shoulder and smiled and waved. "Bye, Lucy." I shouted as I waved my hand high above my head.

I then sat back down on the grass and pulled out a few blades of grass and tossed them into the wind. I looked to my side and noticed Gabbie smiling and staring off into the distance. I called to her and said, "Everything is gonna be okay, Gabs. Sash is with us." She then turned her attention to me, and I leaned forward and pet her gently on her head. I then got up but stayed in a crouch position and sat down next to her. I wiped my hands on my jeans to rid myself of dirt then laid on the grass and put my head on her side. She then my planked over and sprawled out across the grass and shut her eyes.

I laid there without saying a word and stared up into the clear blue sky and watched as a few clouds periodically came into view. Though I was grief stricken and barely able to function I couldn't help but smile as

I suddenly realized Sasha had been right beside me the entire time. I said while looking up into the clouds, "I love you, Sash."

PSLAM OF TRINITY

Before all things began, the Word was there:
one Word of life already, at the world's creation;
for what God was, the Word was also:
rooted and grounded in love, for God is love.

All creation was made by the Word of God:
all love was shown by God, and by that Word on
earth, for through him, God spoke to us:
and, by his Word, God said, "I love you".

The Spirit was there already when all things were
created: your breath moved over the mists at the
world's beginning; since that Spirit is the Spirit of
love: inspiring and encouraging us all,
you are in us always.

So, Creator and Spirit are one: you've been here
since the beginning, and you're also with us, in
loving and creating you are at work: your love
is in us now, through Word and Spirit.

"If I could be half the person my dog is, I'd be twice the human I am."

- Charles Yu

CHAPTER TWENTY
BEFORE EXODUS

Over the weeks and months since Sasha passed away, I had been trying desperately to get back to some kind of normal life. However, it seemed all but impossible. Periodically I had succumbed to an occasional moment of weakness; anger erupted out of every pore of my body; dried tears stuck to my face, and the sadness became so great that all I wanted to do was sleep the days away. One night I found myself rushing to the bathroom and slamming the door shut. I flicked on the light switch and stood before the toilet; I was certain I was going to vomit.

After a few moments I exhaled a long, shallow breath and placed my hands on the edges of the sink. I stood in front of the mirror staring at my reflection. It felt like I was standing there for days but it was no more than two to three minutes. I gritted my teeth and pulled my hands slowly away from the sink edges. I balled my fists and clenched my hands harder and harder into two fists until my fingernails dug deep into the flesh of my palms nearly drawing blood.

The muscles in my arms were straining and I could feel my hands going numb. I raised my fists to my face and shook my arms and then began to cry. I sucked all the breath back into my lungs and forced the tears to stop; I was overwhelmed by rage which was becoming uncontrollable. I grunted and then lashed out and swung my right arm out in front of me striking the mirror over the sink; the glass splintered in all directions and small shards punctured my hand and cut my knuckles. My fist hit the mirror with such force that the wall unit shook loose from the brackets that secured it to the sheetrock. My outburst lasted for only a moment and then my body became weak. I stumbled over to the toilet and sat down and placed my elbows on my knees. I cupped my hands over my face and cried softly at first then hard. I said aloud, "I can't do this without you, Sash." I sniffled and then said, "God, how I miss you, baby girl."

As I sat there sulking, I felt something overcome me. This time it wasn't a ghostly voice or apparition, however, but it was familiar feeling, nonetheless. A memory had flashed in my mind of when I found myself coping with similar circumstances. I began to recall the horrible day when my mother sat on the edge of my bed and said, "Doctor Glatt passed away this morning..." (Doctor Glatt, or Howard was like a second father to me). It had been over a decade since he collapsed from a sudden heart attack, and for some reason I found myself once again making a silent pact like I did all those years prior. This time, as I sat on the toilet seat I spoke aloud and began by saying, "I can't do this without you, girl." I sobbed for a moment. A tear rolled down my cheek and then fell to the ground; it sounded like thunder and the sound echoed in my ears. "What am I gonna do now? "I stood up and then something happened - my grief tuned to anger. But, not normal anger; anger that empowered me. And then I said aloud speaking directly to Sasha, "I will not fail you, Sash." It was a corny and cliché thing to say but it was the truth, nonetheless.

I turned to the sink and opened the cold-water faucet and splashed water on my face. I then opened the bathroom door and found Gabbie lying outside; she was wagging her tail and happy to see me. I kneeled down and lifted her gently off the ground and held her close. I whispered into her ear like I've done for months now and told her, "Sash is with us, Gabs. I promise everything is going to be okay. I love you," I kissed Gabbie on her nose then continued and said, "It's me, you and Sash forever!" I gently placed her on the floor and walked into the living room and sat at my computer. She continued to look at me, however, and then a few moments later she got up and walked to where I was sitting. She sat down at my feet and I pet her on her neck and back.

She turned and looked back at me and smiled. I smiled back and blew her a kiss at her then said, "I will never leave you, girl." I then asked her even though I knew she wouldn't answer me, "You know that, right, Gabs?" She continued to smile at me. I watched as her tongue then fell out of the side of her mouth and drool dripped on the floor. I chuckled a few times and then leaned forward and rubbed her behind her ears. "Baby girl," I said. "I'll find a way. I promise." I relaxed against the back of the couch and took a deep breath and said softly, "Somehow we will escape this Hell."

I looked down as I felt Gabbie rest her head on my leg; I could sense she was worried about me. We locked eyes for a moment, and I told her reassuringly, "I won't give up." I sat there motionless and deep in thought. Roughly fifteen minutes later I felt myself drifting off in an awkward state of sleep as if I was being hypnotized. I slept through the night with Gabbie laying comfortably at my feet. I can't recall and notable dreams or jaw dropped spiritual experiences. However, something happened to me while I was sound asleep. Whatever occurred had altered me drastically.

The following morning, I awoke and began to put my plan into motion. Two days later I would be well on my way to finding the answers I was searching for. However, unbeknownst to me it wasn't me who was doing the searching. I would later come to find out that just as desperate as I was to find the means to change my life there was someone else who lived one three thousand miles away who was trying to locate my whereabouts. As time went on, we drew closer and closer to discovering each other existence. But, how would we finally find one another? However, even if we did find one another would I really be able to travel such a far distance with no car and very little money? Well, whether you choose to believe it or not that was the easy part...

...whoops! I'm ruining the story. Let me stick with the past and present before jumping to the future. Fair? Okay, now, where was I?

PSALM 126

When the LORD restored the fortunes of Zion, we were like those who dreamed.

Our mouths were filled with laughter, our tongues with songs of joy. Then it was said among the nations, "The LORD has done great things for them."

The LORD has done great things for us, and we are filled with joy.

Restore our fortunes, LORD, like streams in the Negev. Those who sow with tears will reap with songs of joy.

Those who go out weeping, carrying seed to sow, will return with songs of joy, carrying sheaves with them.

"We have a queen-size bed, and the dog sleeps in the middle. John and I are sort of these little quotation marks on either corner."

- Rachael Ray

CHAPTER TWENTY-ONE
PAIN IS A PRISON

The day was cool and breezy. I wanted to get out of the house so I decided to go to the other side of town where I could find peace of mind (or so I hoped); my neighborhood was overrun by the sounds of speeding buses and honking horns. I sat on the brick states of an apartment building which was directly across from my friend's house and a few blocks from where I once lived. I stared at the people boarding the bus and was overcome by a feeling pity. For some reason I was watching them and trying to understand why they did what they did? Were they going to work? Were they sightseeing? Or perhaps they just wanted to enjoy the weather? However, none of these answers made any sense to me. For the first time in over a decade I didn't understand what was so special about being alive? Just like all those years prior I once again found myself thinking, What the fuck I am doing? Life is so damn pointless. Even today I can remember the array of unanswerable questions that zipped through my brain as I tried to find a reason to not jump in front of an on-coming bus. I dwelled on thoughts of my family, my friends and all those that have been helping me since all this began. I told myself, "Whether I want to or not I have to live. I have to make things right. After that who knows?"

I must have sat on the steps of a random apartment complex hours. I pretended that I lived there while all the while smoking one cigarette after another. I found myself deep in thought and recalling events which what had transpired over the past few years; events that were both good and bad. Yet, the more I began to think the more I began to hate myself. I endlessly wished that I could take back the hurt and pain I caused many people, even my own family. I concluded that what I was experiencing was somehow my penance. However, it was unjust punishment and borderline inhuman treatment of a man who was trying to rebuild his life the only way he knew how. It was then that something clicked inside me. Something that drove me to search harder and harder for an exit out of the Hell that I found myself trapped in.

It seemed that there was a chain if events that unfolded right before my eyes and it began when I started to wonder about the people who passed me by without even a second glance. I thought hard and long about what, if anything was important to these people who casually entered and exited the bus which was stopped on the street corner? I exhaled smoke from my nostrils and said to myself, "These people are fucking clueless." I then stood up and dropped my cigarette to the ground and crushed it under my shoe and walked up the sidewalk the turned toward the deli; I wanted a coffee.

I entered the deli and spotted a man who's name I didn't know but who was always excited when I brought Sasha by spend time with him; he was a scruffy with gray hair. I entered the deli and he immediately asked how I was doing. I sulked and shrugged my shoulders then told him, "There's not a day that goes by when I don't miss her." He patted me on the shoulder and replied, "Anyone would agree that you gave her an amazing life." I looked up at him and smiled; I was hiding my tears. "No matter how hard things got, no matter how little you think you did for her no one could have done better!" He lowered his arm and I extended my hand out in front of me. He gently shook my hand and I told him thank you.

We spoke for another ten minutes and then I left. I sipped on my coffee and began to walk back to the building where I was making camp. However, as I turned the corner, I became dizzy and nearly feel face first onto the concrete; I was still having a momentary relapse of vertigo. My coffee spilled over the brim of the cup but strangely I didn't flinch (or even cringe) from the boiling liquid that was scolding my hand. Then, from over my shoulder a familiar voice called out; it was my friend who lived in a nearby apartment complex. He shouted at me and told me to come to him. I tried hard not to show him I was in pain and quickly regained my composure and carefully crossed the street.

I got within arm's reach of my friend and he snapped his arm out in front of him and grabbed me by my shoulder and pulled me close to him and gave a hug. He patted me on the back then let go of me and said, "How you doing?" I nodded and avoided eye contact with him; he knew that things weren't as good as he hoped they were. I stood there in front of him and listened as he told me, "Leave this place..." I interrupted him and in a defiant voice said, "I can't. If I leave, I leave her." I took a cigarette out of the box and placed it in my mouth then light it. I looked at my friend and said while puffing on my cigarette, "Believe it as much as I hate this place I have to stay." My friend seemed to scold me with his eyes as replied, "Sasha wants you to be happy." I dropped the cigarette on the ground after taking only another few small puffs on it and crushed it under my shoe, "I know. But, without her I can never be happy." He shook his head, "You're so stubborn sometimes." We laughed in unison. He then continued, "I know you feel that this is your home..." Again, I interrupted him. "Look there." I said while turning slightly back over my shoulder and pointing to a reinforced iron fence outside the deli which lead into the basement. "Yea," he replied. "What about it?" He asked. I lowered my arm and turned back to face him. "That was her spot." He raised one corner of his mouth and cracked a small smile, "And it always will be."

I said nothing and turned away from my friend and looked out into the street when a quick memory of Sasha popped into my mind. I remembered back to a day when the sun was shining, and it was early morning. It was spring (or about to be) and I was going to the deli to get my morning coffee. I decided to take Sasha for a quick walk. She was pulling hard against the leash trying to hurry me to her favorite spot outside the deli. I smiled then turned fully around and looked at my friend who was anticipating the words that I would speak next.

I put my hands in my pant pockets and looked him in the eyes while asking him, "Do you care about me?" He blurted out without any hesitation at all and said, "Of course!" He seemed insulted by my question and continued, asking, "What kind of question is that?" He scoffed, "You know I love you." I looked into his eyes and asked him, "And what does the word "love" mean to you?" He furrowed his brow and replied inquisitively, "Drew? What the Hell are you getting at?" He stepped forward and continued, "You're blind. Just like the rest of them." I took my hands out of my pockets and handed him a medallion that I had carried with me for weeks; it was a gift given to me by a member of my support group with a paw print and heart stamped into it. He took the medallion and inspected it carefully. "What's this?" He asked while handing the mediation back to me. "I knew you wouldn't understand." I told him.

After a few moments of deep thought, he moved towards a nearby railing and while placing on hand on the railing he said, "I don't get it?" I chuckled softly and smirked. "Don't worry..." I then began to walk back up the sidewalk. I continued and said, "I'm sure one day you will." He seemed anxious and I could sense he had worry in his voice as he asked me, "Where are you going?" I said nothing as I continued to walk up the sidewalk to the top of the hill. I took a cigarette out of the pack which was stuffed into my front pant pocket and placed it between my lips and let it dangle from the side of my mouth. I mumbled incoherent babble then light the cigarette and inhaled once. I said in a soft voice with smoke coming out my mouth and nostrils, "Nothing you do can make me break my promise."

I stopped at the corner and looked up at the crosswalk sign while casually smoking my cigarette and waiting for the light to change from red to green. I was startled when a middle-aged woman appeared like a ghost next to me. She at me strangely as if I was clinically insane; she must have seen me talking to myself? I turned to face her and said hello and smiled warmly. Just then the crosswalk sign then changed to green and I walked across the street to the other side. I turned sideways into the direction of the sun and looked up in the clear blue sky. I then tossed the cigarette into a small puddle of muddy water in front of me and walked to the adjacent building while dwelling on the future.

The rest of the day was filled with an array of up and down emotions which filled me with nausea. Later that night I got a call from my father. At the start of the conversation he asked me, "What are you up to?" I replied quickly, "Thinking." I could hear a commotion in the background behind him; it was my nephews playing. I was distant as my father said into the phone receiver, "Don't let the pain eat away at you." He paused as one of my nephews shouted for him to hang up the phone and come play with him. I sighed in a heavy breath, "Pain is all I have, dad." He seemed distracted but quickly became re-engaged in our conversation, "You need to find a way to get passed it." I combed one hand through my hair and replied, "I know you don't understand, dad, and that's okay. All you need to know is that II need this pain."

I looked out the window of my room and up into the blackness of the night. He became frustrated with my remarks but remained calm and collected; I assumed he didn't want to upset me? "No one needs pain, son. It's unhealthy." He said to me in a fatherly voice while hiding his frustration. I took the phone from my ear and rolled my head to one side; my muscles in my neck were becoming cramped. "Dad, pain is part of life. It's how a person deals with that makes them weak or strong." My riddles seemed to always confuse him. He asked, "What does that mean?" I gritted my teeth and replied, "I won't be weak, dad He tried to speak but I spoke over him and continued, saying, "My pain is all that keeps me alive." I could hear him sigh as he said, "I'm worried about you, son." I blurted out, "There's nothing to worry about, dad. I promise."

A crackle overcame the phone; the connection was fading. "I know how much you love Sasha. Don't dishonor her memory by trying to change..." He stopped speaking as he heard me chuckle softly; I was thinking he was repeating something I had written in one of my former books? "You're starting to sound like me, ya know that?" I could sense he was smiling as he replied, "I've been reading too many of your books, I guess?" I smacked my lips, "Stop bullshitting!" I then laughed. "You never read one book I've ever written." He interjected and playfully remarked, "That's a lie!" I contained my laughter as I heard him continue, saying, "Well, I did read about half of the last one you wrote; but it was morbid." I couldn't contain my laughter anymore and moments later burst out into hysterics.

A few moments later I said goodnight to him but as I did, he said into the phone, "Son," I stopped and placed the phone closer to my ear. He then said, "Don't let pain become a prison." I agreed with him (even though I disagreed with him). Before he hung up the phone, I told him, "Dad, I know I must sound like a broken record, but I really do love you, all of you. I'm sorry for hurting everyone and letting you all down." He didn't say much other then, "Just remember what I told you." My voice was filled with sadness; I was recalling hurtful memories. I then asked him, "You said a lot of things. Remind me…" His stubble scratched the phone as he replied, "Don't turn to the dark side. Don't become Darth Vader." I laughed and then a smile streaked across my face and I replied, "I won't. Just don't give up me. Okay?" He yawned and then told me boldly, "I won't, and I never have." Hearing him say that re-kindled the fire which was slowly being extinguished inside me by an unknown force.

Following my conversation with my father from the night prior I kept all my emotions from him. I never again let him know when I had cried nor when I am having a shitty day. Instead I continued to remind him that I would overcome and defeat the sadness and conquer the grief. I know it was not appropriate to trick him into believing that I was recuperating but I had no choice. I was certain that if he dwelled on me and worried endlessly, I would inadvertently strip him of his happiness, and that was something I couldn't allow to happen.

Shortly thereafter I called him and told him, "Dad, I did it! I'm moving." He was surprised and asked, "To where?" And I told him without hesitation, "I tell you when I get there." His voice was shaky as he replied, "Is everything okay?" I smiled and told him happily, "Everything is fine." I continued, saying, "Trust me, dad. Six months from now it will be like none of this every happened." I picked up my coffee mug that was next to my bed and took a sip then continued, "I will keep my promise..." I placed the cup of coffee back down on the table and continued and told him confidently, "To you, mom, to everyone!" I then snatched a cigarette from the pack which was laying still next to my coffee mug and put in my mouth and finished by saying, "And, of course, for Sash and Gabs."

I nearly cried as I listened to him say, "I'm proud of you, son." However, I could feel tears swell in my eyes and I tried hard to hold them back. I swallowed hard and replied, "That's all I ever wanted." I then listened as he told me, "Give Gabbie a kiss for me." I replied quickly, "I will." I then said goodbye to him and as I hung up the phone he interjected and said, "Call me from the road and tell me everything is alright." I smoked my cigarette and replied, "I will, dad. Promise." Before he allowed me to hang up, he said one last thing. "Just don't be afraid to tell me what's really going on?" I cleared my throat; the smoke had itched my esophagus then replied, "Dad, things will be different. You'll see." Silence overtook the air. Then, suddenly he blurted out and said, "I believe you."

It had been a long time since my father, and I spoke with yelling at one another. For the first time in a long time I felt happy. I finally felt like I was on the cusp of greatness. Yet, as I would soon come to learn greatness was only the beginning.

"Ever wonder where you'd end up if you took your dog for a walk and never once pulled back on the leash?"

- Robert Brault

CHAPTER TWENTY - TWO
ALL YOU NEED IS FAITH

Trying to figure out a way to end this book with closure for you, the reader was a difficult task. As a matter of fact, I wrote and re-wrote this chapter but inevitably deleted the majority of the paragraphs I had to committed to using a means to end this book. However, over the weeks I chose to delete those paragraphs and start over. To be honest I felt as if they were unbecoming of the ending to such a fantastic story. What I chose to do instead was to finish this book by staring the next one, or rather give you an excerpt from the upcoming novella, The WheelHouse: Part 1.5: The Missing Pieces.

Before doing so I want to assure you that The Journey Back is not as morbid as the book you are now reading. Perhaps that statement is unfair? In fact, morbid is the wrong word to use. Let me rephrase that by saying that the events of this book served as a roadmap of sorts which would eventually unraveled a puzzle which I have been trying to solve since the day I conceived conscious thought. You're confused, aren't you? In time you won't be, I promise.

I won't divulge too many details to you about what transpired over the coming months (it would ruin the surprise). Yet, what I will tell you is this - faith is all you need to find what you are looking whether it be something you seek in this world or quite possibly the next. You may be asking, "What is faith exactly?" Truthfully, there are an insurmountable number of people of think that they know the definition of faith but are sorely mistaken. To understand faith why don't you first recall from memory the story of Abraham? Ring any bells? Unfortunately, I won't waste time repeating what is readily available to you in the Bible. So, if you don't know the story that I am referring to then just simply open the Bible or even Google the scripture online…Let me continue, shall I?...

One day in mid-November of 2015 I decided to go for a walk to try to gather my thoughts. After a while I found myself seventeen miles away from home. It was then that I realized that I was in trouble. I had no money, no water or food and my cell phone had only one bar of battery left. I began to notice that my legs had become incredibly cramped which had forced me to collapse on the side of the highway. I sat there in excruciating pain and barely able to move. I was hoping that someone would stop to help me but, no one did; it was New York after all, and a good Samaritan was rare if not unheard of. However, as I shut my eyes and allowed the pain to overcome my body, she came back to me.

Wait! I'm getting ahead of myself. Let me go back to earlier that morning when a feeling overcame me which forced me to stare out my bedroom window and into the busy street. I would periodically look up into the clear blue sky but had no idea why I was doing so in the first place. I thought of these moments from earlier that morning as I sat on the side of the highway curled up in a fetal position and trying to stay warm. Suddenly, the same sensation I felt while staring out into the busy street again overcame me. What happened next may sound too good to be true to some readers, but I assure this is no tall tale. I felt the strange sensation overcome. I struggled to raise myself up off the grassy knoll. I called out but no one was there. I sat on my knees and a squinted my eyes; I tried to focus on the darkness to reveal anyone (or thing) who could have been hiding nearby. I was flabbergasted; I gasped and feel back onto my hands. A figure appeared a few feet away. It was here - Sasha. Though, seconds later she vanished. I thought I was hallucinating and told myself to get up and find help as quickly as possible. But, then from out of the darkness I hear her; calling to me with a loud bark that echoed all around me. I called her name and as I greeted her the pain in my legs subsided and I was filled with an energy I never had before. Then, a vision flashed before me, but it was hard to decipher; sort of like a jigsaw puzzle. Next, the vision vanished just as quickly as it appeared. I called for Sasha, but I heard nothing; just then sound of a speeding car off in the distance broke the silence.

I tried to regain my composure but was distracted by an ominous chill that ran through my entire body. I shook uncontrollably and I felt like I was being watched, "Who's there?" I asked loudly. I stood up and as I did, I felt like I had been transported somewhere else; to a strange world beyond my imagination. I stood still engulfed by the darkness and strangely I felt protected. A few seconds passed and I shook my head violently and tried hard to focus on where I was and how I would find rescue. However, I couldn't stop thinking about what had just happened. In fact, I was adamant that this vision was showing me the future. I had become convinced that a day would come when I would be compelled to quickly grab Gabbie and my belongings, leave me apartment without notice, and get in a car and travel thousands of miles to an unknown destination.

I knew I needed to get to place where I could find help. I forced myself to continue walking through the blackness of the night. I walked about a half mile when I slumped over a guard rail and collapsed onto my hands and knees. I laid still on a patch of grass all the while trying to conceal myself in the shadows; I was cold and all I wanted to do was sleep. I must have laid there on the grass for forty-five minutes before my eyes sprung open and I suddenly remembered Gabbie; she had been alone for nearly a full day now. Yet, I was certain she was in much better condition than I was. Still, I worried about her immensely.

I pushed myself up off the grassy knoll and realized my legs were completely unusable; the soreness was crippling. For the next three hours I would say nothing, not even smoke a cigarette as a matter of fact. My thoughts dwelled on Gabbie and I used every ounce of my remaining strength to keep walking; I had to get back to her no matter the cost. I walked for about a mile before I saw streetlights illuminate the asphalt and the rays of light glisten off the wet pavement (at least I thought it was wet). I then spotted a gas station and from the look of things the station appeared to still be open; it was now close to three o'clock in the morning.

As I got near to the gas station I sighed with relief. Yet, there was no one in sight and the only sound I heard was crickets and an occasional bullfrog which croaked loudly from the nearby sump. I walked to the corner of the road when I saw a police car pull into the gas station and parked under a light. I sped up my walk and hoped that I would get there in time before the police car left again. There were no cars in sight, so I decided not to wait for the crosswalk signal. As I got near to the police car, I could see a female police officer sitting in the driver's seat thumbing through a stack of papers in her lap. He ruled the down the window and asked me to stop and then demanded to know what I was doing. I breathed heavy and replied, "I need to get home." She seemed confused and asked me, "Do you have a car?" I looked at her and shook my head no. "How did you get all the way out here?" She asked curiously. I stepped back and leaned up against a dumpster. "I walked." I told her.

She opened the door and with one hand on her gun harness asked inquisitively, "From where?" I chuckled and replied, "You won't believe me if I told you." She held out one hand and asked me for my I.D. I carefully took my wallet out of my back pocket and gently placed it in her hand. She opened and took out my license and asked rhetorically, "Florida? Are you telling me you walked all the way here from Florida?" She handed me back my wallet and I replied, "Queens, actually." She seemed agitated. "You should have just told me that in the first place," she said angrily. I stood upright and felt my legs shake and asked her, "Can you drive me back? I really need to get home." She got back in her police cruiser and said, "I can only take you as far as Main Street." I smiled and replied, "I'm fine with that. My house isn't too far from Main Street, actually."

I got in the back of the police cruiser and felt relived. After a moment or two she began to make small talk and again asked me how I ended up so far from home? I told her it was a long story and she would rather not know. However, something odd happened next. Without any coaxing whatsoever she began to tell me that she had eight dogs at home. Even stranger was that she told me that she had a five-year-old Boxer. I was shocked. I gawked at her and then explained how I had just lost Sasha to cancer, and even mentioned that I thought it was ironic that I would meet her and discover she too had a Boxer; maybe it wasn't ironic after all. It was then that had transpired that evening finally made sense.

She dropped me off on the corner of Main Street and told me goodbye and good luck. I thanked her for the ride and assured her I would get home just fine. I walked for about another hour until I finally reached the front door to my apartment. My heart was racing as I opened the door; I was worried about Gabbie and that something may have happened to her while I was away. However, to my surprise she was lying right where I had left her - next to Sasha's urn. I called to her and smiled then collapsed onto the couch. She turned to look back at me then rolled over and up. She stared at me; her gaze made me worry. I asked her, "Gabs? You okay, girl?" In the blink of any eye she used her snout and pushed her food bowl too my feet. I laughed loudly and told her, "I should have known." I got up from the couch and walked to the bag of food wedged between the dresser and wall. I took scoops of food and emptied into the bowl then put in down in front of Gabbie. It took her seconds to devour it. I sat back down on the couch and shut my eyes. "I'm gonna get some sleep, okay, Gabs?" I then opened my eyes slightly and saw her starting at me with a streaking smile on her face. I laid down with my head on one armrest and feet on another and told her, "I love you, Gab, Gab."

I'm not sure how long I was asleep for, but it felt like days. When I finally awoke, I was groggy and sorer than ever before. It was hard for me to move my legs nonetheless stand up or walk. Later that day I got a phone call from a producer in Los Angeles. I remember the conversation started with, "Would you be willing to come here if I gave you a place to stay?" I eagerly replied, "Of course!" I then passed momentarily. I remembered the vision I had from the a few nights prior. "It can't be!" I thought. I then continue and told her, "As long as Gabbie come, that is. I won't go anywhere without her. She asked me curiously, "Who's Gabbie." I responded quickly, "My dog." She exclaimed, "I love dogs! I have three!"

Roughly a minute later my phone vibrated alerting me to a new text message. I was still speaking with the producer but took the phone away from my ear to see who it was. I opened the text message and saw a picture of three dogs. I smiled and told her, "I just got your text." She happily replied, "Great!" I then said, "They're cute!" She asked me, "Will Gabbie get along with them?" I scoffed and replied, "Gabbie will love them!"

It was about week later when I packed my belongings and asked Gabbie, "You want to go to California, Gabs?" I remember she looked up at me as if to say, "Yes, as long as we never have to come back to this shit hole." I pet her gently and continued telling her, "Everything's gonna be okay, Gab, Gab. I promise." I remember it was cold and rainy that day. I was being picked up by a total stranger and oddly I had no fear. However, I continued to think about how all these events unfolded in the first place. I remembered back to the night I was near death and lying lifeless on the side of the highway. As you may recall it was there when I first had the vision which showed me that I would soon be leaving this retched city. Until now I found it hard it believe at all. Yet, what was even more unbelievable was how it now appeared that someone (or something) was guiding me on a new journey; yet what journey was yet to be seen. Still, I wondered who was behind it all? Was it God or someone else? Only one name came to mind - Sasha.

I was sitting at home and watching Netflix when my phone rang; it four o'clock in the afternoon. I answered and said hello. I listened as a woman who I never spoke to before told me she had found me through a mutual contact we both met off Craigslist (and people say Craigslist is bad). Originally, I was supposed to drive a car from New York to San Francisco for a gentleman who was flying back home to California for the holidays and didn't want to transport his car by freight.

A few days earlier I agreed to drive the car but came to realize that my license was suspend. I was about to give up hope of ever getting to the West Coast. However, it was then that a miracle had happened. Since I was unable to drive the car the gentlemen who hired me inevitably hired someone new. Yet, due to a miscommunication she thought I was still driving the car and initially asked me if she could tag along. After explaining to her that my license was suspended, she asked me, "Well, do you still want to go?" I excitedly replied, "Of course! But I'm not leaving my dog." She laughed and said, "I understand. Besides, my dogs could use the company." It turned out that she was bringing her two dogs as well. It seemed too good to be true. I then gave her my address and she agreed to pick me up two days later. I told her that if she drove, I would pay gas, tolls and hotels; It seemed only fair.

As the days passed, I found myself eagerly awaiting her phone call. Finally, she had called and asked, "Can you be ready to leave tomorrow?" I said without hesitation, "I could be ready to leave today if we had to!" The following day she was scheduled to pick me and Gabbie up. I found myself waiting on the curb outside my apartment and looking up to see that the sky was overcast. A few moments later my eyes shifted to the bust street before me. I stood in the cold looking down the street trying hard to spot her car. About fifteen minutes passed and suddenly my phone rang. My teeth chattered as I said, "Hello?" I then listened as she told me she was fifteen minutes away and asked me to meet her out front with Gabbie. I told her no problem and began to move my bags downstairs.

I left Gabbie in the apartment for the time being because I didn't want her to get wet in the rain. I remember standing int the living room watching Gabbie drink water. I kneeled next to her and pet her gently on the top of her head and told her, "There's no turning back now, Gabs." She seemed uninterested in what I had to say and continued to drink water. I didn't mind that she did since it would be hours before she would be able to have any more.

Finally, my ride had come. I ran back inside and picked up Gabbie and cradled her in my arms. "Here we go, Gabs!" Told her happily. I then rushed her downstairs and hurried to the car to see that it was van. "Roomy, huh, Gabs?" After a brief introduction I placed Gabbie in the van and then began to pack my suitcase and garbage bags full of dirt clothes into the back. Shortly after I jumped into the van and planked myself down in seat next to Gabbie then closed the door. A few minutes later the lady who so graciously offered me a ride got into the front seat and excitedly said, "Okay! We're off!" I smiled and then asked her if I could smoke a cigarette and she replied, "Only if I can have one?" I chuckled and replied, "No problem." I took a cigarette out of the pack and handed it to her. "You like Reds? She replied, "There's nothing better." I then light my cigarette and smoked it slowly.

As we began to drive down the road, I took one last look through the rear windshield of the car and muttered the words, "This time it's forever." I turned to Gabbie who was lying asleep on the floor next to me. I reached forward and pet her gently on the top of her head trying not to wake her and whispered, "I love you, Gabs." She opened her eyes and turned her head then looked up at me. With ease she laid her head against my leg. "Everything is gonna be okay, baby girl," I told her reassuringly. I then leaned back into the seat and shut my eyes. I took a deep breath and then smiled out of the corner of my mouth.

I listened as the sounds of the city faded away and silence overtook the air. Again, I looked down at Gabbie who was relaxed and peaceful and lying silently at my feet. I smiled and told her again, "I love you, Gabbers." She raised her head slightly off my leg and her tongue fell out of the corner of her mouth; she was panting. "You hot girl?" I asked her. I reached forward and pet her gently on her belly. She then rested her head on the floor of the van shut her eyes. "Good idea, Gabs," I said aloud. "Let's get some sleep. We got a long ride ahead of us." I crossed my arms in front of me to keep warm then. A few seconds later the sun hit my face warming my skin slightly. I kept my eyes shut but turned to face the window; I could feel Sasha's presence all around me. I then opened my eyes and muttered, "I love you too, Sash. I miss you."

As the massive skyscrapers, roaring planes and screaming ambulances became non-existent I somehow knew things were going to be different. However, change can be frightening. The future wasn't written. I couldn't stop thinking if everything would turn out okay. Endless thoughts raced through my head and I questioned would this time be no different than all the others? Were me and Gabbie going to be safe? I had no idea. But, one thing was for certain - whatever happened would happen to both of us; Gabbie and I.

As I was trying to fall asleep the driver of the car called back to me and asked if I would be bothered if she tuned on the radio? I replied to her, "No problem." She then turned the dial on the radio and to my surprise I heard the song, "Here I go again" by Whitesnake play through the speakers. I became excited and laughed in amusement. The driver called back to me and asked if I was okay? I told her I was fine and explained how ironic it was that that song would play at that exact moment. In fact, this wasn't the first time this happened to me as you might recall. I leaned forward and asked her rhetorically, "Don't you think it's weird how the universe gives you signs to tell you everything will be okay?"

I took a cigarette out of the pack that was resting next to the window and then relaxed in my seat which felt like a plank of solid wood; the springs were protruding into my back and the seat cushion was caved in. At first, she (the driver of the car) said nothing but after a few moments she looked back at me and while holding the steering wheel firmly in both hands she replied, "The weird part would be not knowing when it did." She then smirked as if she knew something I didn't then turned back to focus on driving. That night I texted my father and wrote, "I about thirty minutes outside of Pennsylvania." He wrote back moments later, "Where are you headed?" I muttered softly, "You never did like surprises, did ya, dad?"

The woman driving turned slightly and asked me, "You say something?" I looked up and replied, "Oh, my bad. I was talking to my dad." She returned to driving and I continued to write a text to my father. I wrote, "Like I told you - I'll tell you when I get there." He quickly answered back, "You know I don't like surprises." I smirked and spoke out loud but kept me voice low, so the driver of the car didn't mistake me talking to her. "My thoughts exactly, dad." I then wrote him back and ended our conversation with, "Don't worry. Everything will be okay." A minute or two later my phone vibrated, and I was alerted to a new text from my father. It read, "Goodnight, Son. I'm proud of you."

I wrote him back and told him I loved him, and I would be in touch soon. I leaned forward and placed my hand on the headrest of the driver's seat and asked, "How long till where get there you think?" The woman replied, "About five days..." My eyes widened, "No shit!" I looked down at Gabbie and pet on her gently on her head and said, "We're on our way, baby girl. We're on our way." I looked out the window and continued, saying in a low almost muffled voice, "We did it!" I then shut my eyes and began to doze off; softly falling into a peaceful slumber.

THREE HEARTS. ONE SOUL.

*I called His name and I heard Him whisper, "The time
is nigh for you must wait." I denied my brethren
while I searched for answers. The answers
He said, "Will come from three."*

*Then one day I heard Him say, "I have sent you two
angels for you to find. To do so you must open
your eyes." I searched for you but to no avail;
tired and hungry I looked high and low;
waiting for sign of your arrival.*

*Then one day I saw your face; that was the day
I changed my fate. You looked at me with
innocent eyes; I looked back at you and you
showed me another; never speaking
a word only staring at one other.*

*They call you dogs, but I call you my daughters;
you are all that matter. They know not who
we are, but we are known by many.*

*They look for miracles above and below. Their eyes
are clouded; the miracles come and go. What we
know they will never hear; what we are they
will never be.*

*Then He called down and said to us three, "By fire
and fright I will test your faith." We looked up
at Him and He continued to say, "At the end
of the night the light shall fade. Fear not
the dark because you are
the way."*

*It was on that day that our souls became one.
We traveled afar seeking others to join us. In time
we saw what He was trying to show us. Then
one day we heard Him say, "Follow the light
and you shall find the way."*

*We returned to our home where others found us.
Still, he told us, "You must find the way." We
watched them pass while others remained. We
then said to each other, "We are one,
we are forever."*

*Thunder cracked and lightning exploded. His
voice then echoed, "You have found the way!"
We smiled to each other and said to
those who remained, "The time has come
for us to lead the way."*

\- a poem by Drew Glick

FINAL THOUGHTS

For those people out there that will inevitably ask, "Drew, will you ever get another dog?" the answer is, no. Some people may say that my view will change over time, but you are sorely mistaken. Whether you want to say that I am exaggerating or not believe me when I say that every dog owner will tell you the same thing, "I feel as if I lost a child." Therefore, as a parent (if you are a parent, that is) you wouldn't rush to conceive another child, would you? So, why would it be expected for me (or anyone) to get a dog that could never replace those that I lost?

Dogs are not decorations for our home. I think it is time that the human race opens its eyes to see the value of life. We (humanity) have an indomitable spirit, an unbreakable will, supreme intellect, and yet with all of this might we still only care about one thing - ourselves. The sad truth is that until we as a species begin to see the value of not only our lives, but the of the all the inhabitants of earth we will never truly understand why we are here in the first place. I hope for those of you who read this book you will see that there is more to life than what you think you know. Though, I'm being repetitive let me say it again: life is not about "things" but rather about happiness. If you asked me, "Drew, you seem to know it all. So, tell me how I achieve happiness?" I would answer you by saying, "The only way you know how." Surely you would be confused by this remark. Or would you? I am assuming you are an intelligent person if you are reading this book? Therefore, you wouldn't be confused and maybe you already know what I am telling you? Yet, happiness comes with a price; nothing in life is free. To achieve what you desire most you must fight for what or who you love. This is why we live. This is why we struggle.

Our existence, this moment, and the years of our lives which we spend pursuing the things which make us happy serve only one purpose - to determine our place in the afterlife. You don't agree, do you? Think about it. The Bible says it. The Torah speaks of it too. You still don't know what I am talking about do you? Let me say this in layman's terms: we, human beings are here to earn the right to have a soul; to move on to the plain of enlightenment, in other words.

Let me give you an example to help put what I am saying into a better perspective. Recently, I saw a film that I forget existed. It's called, "Defending Your Life" and stars *Meryl Streep* and *Albert Brooks*. While watching it I came to realize that I wasn't the only person who believed that our deeds in this life determine whether we "move forward or return to earth to try again." The film depicts many things but one notable and obvious point to the film was that - our life choices are like fuel that moves our soul and gives our soul a type of unconscious intelligence

Ask yourself: What kind of person am I? Would you see your life as wasted if you took on the burdens of other people, or even animals for that matter? Would you feel regret if you spent your life savings to help a dog defeat cancer? If you answered "no" to any of the questions, then let me be the first person to welcome you to the human race. If you answered "yes" then you are not worthy of the love you so badly desire. Yes, love, what else did you think I was referring to? Wait! Don't tell me that the word "love" is taboo or something, and for shit's sake stop acting as if "love" is wasted energy or an annoyance of some kind that only ends in despair.

Maybe you're quietly saying, "But, Drew look at all the dumb ass shit you went through while in a relationship." Maybe it was stupid? But, regardless of what the relationship "was" in the end I found what I was looking for; I found my soulmates (even if they do have shaggy fur and short tails). It is important that people like us, animal lovers specifically, never allow the outside world to belittle the love that dogs, cats, birds, horses, snakes and so on can give us, human beings, rather. Like I said earlier - the love which animals give human beings is the true definition of the word "unconditional." Remember that and maybe you won't end up like the girl in my story?

I do want to say that the word "dog" is degrading. Let me remind you that Sasha and Gabbie are not "dogs." They are selfless creatures who are more human than most humans are. You see, it is not the word human that makes you or I, or anyone alive today, well, human. It's our love, our ability to understand, our loyalty, our sacrifice and our compassion. No matter what I did, how much I yelled, or how angry I became, Sasha and Gabbie never left me, they never harbored hate or animosity towards me, and they protected me even when I didn't need protecting. Nor did they ever abandon me or choose to deny me because of a grudge. I used to ask myself why? The reason, of course, was obvious - because they love me. Therefore, I have always sacrificed for them no matter the cost, why I continued to love them even when I had no love to give, feed them while I starved and suffered in agony. If you ask me all human beings should aspire to be a dog.

Until next time,

Drew Glick

Drew Glick

-

Dedicated to:
OSCAR, CHEWIE, BAILEY & LADY

The Pack is Complete

Made in the USA
San Bernardino, CA
04 May 2020